The first edition of this book was a game changer for many education leaders, especially for me. The second edition is even more insightful, in that it merges the moral imperative with courage, research, and pragmatism. This book will help transition leaders from being effective to exceptional. A must read!

—*Ron Canuel, Former CEO of Canadian Education Association*

Everything about this astonishing Change Culture revisited is timely, insightful, and compelling. Michael Fullan cuts deeply by having us discover present change leadership challenges while weaving far-reaching answers from education and business practitioners as well as his own personal wisdom. Through *Leading in a Culture of Change, Second Edition*, Fullan takes another leap forward by helping us navigate this current omnipresent complexity of change. A must read!

—*Dr. Bill Hogarth, consultant and former director of education, York Region District School Board*

With accelerating complexity, *Leading in a Culture of Change* is the new normal. In this updated edition, Michael Fullan notes that the more complex the change, the more people must be part of the solution. Like the first edition, moral purpose is job one, but this edition makes it clear that relationships are a close second. This new edition contains many fresh insights as it describes leading from the middle, listening, co-learning, and sense making—all part of the new leadership. The update is as valuable as the first edition was almost two decades ago.

—*Tom Vander Ark, CEO, Getting Smart*

The education sector is so full of change today, it can seem overwhelming to students, parents, teachers and administrators alike. Yet it often feels like we aren't moving anywhere fast – many students and teachers are disengaged with the way they are learning and the leadership they are being provided. In this revised edition of *Leading in a Culture of Change*, Fullan shows us that to make real impact in this context, we must learn to 'go slow to go fast'. This means taking the time to deeply engage with context so that we can become lead learners within our organizations. As Fullan shows, the insights and ideas apply equally to leaders in business and education. Whether you are a leader in a large system, an advisor, or practitioner on the ground, I highly recommend this thought-provoking and practical book to help you in taking the next step forward.

—*William Gort, professional economist and education sector consultant, Deloitte Access Economics*

Fullan delivers a brilliant and compelling strategy for increasing leadership effectiveness. The continual efforts to pursue moral purpose, understand the change process, develop grounded collaboration, foster deep learning knowledge, strive for coherence, and do so with energy, courage, and relentlessness are imperative as educators endeavor to prove that demographics do not determine destiny. *Leading in a Culture of Change, Second Edition,* is the gold standard for addressing the tools necessary to build a solid foundation for effective improvement efforts on behalf of students across all boundaries.

—*Sandy Thorstenson, former superintendent, Whittier Union High School District*

One of the many mistakes I made during my career as a school superintendent was not to place enough emphasis on 'culture' in the 'early' years. I started leading school districts in 1983, and it was Fullan's 2001 book, *Leading in a Culture of Change,* that helped me understand the link between culture and high, continuous, improvement. It was my 'cultural' savior! The second edition is even better. Unlike most business books, Fullan shows how to create, nurture, and benefit from a great culture. Today's young group of leaders do not know what they do not know. If you want to thrive and survive, read *Leading in a Culture of Change.*

—*Dr. Terry Grier, retired superintendent, Houston Independent School District*

LEADING
IN A CULTURE OF
CHANGE

Second Edition

MICHAEL FULLAN

JB JOSSEY-BASS™
A Wiley Brand

Published by Jossey-Bass
A Wiley Brand
111 River St, Hoboken, NJ 07030
www.josseybass.com

Jossey-Bass books and products are available through most bookstores. To contact Jossey-Bass directly call our Customer Care Department within the U.S. at 800-956-7739, outside the U.S. at 317-572-3986, or fax 317-572-4002.

Wiley also publishes its books in a variety of electronic formats and by print-on-demand. For more information about Wiley products, visit www.wiley.com.

Library of Congress Cataloging-in-Publication Data

Names: Fullan, Michael, author.
Title: Leading in a culture of change / Michael Fullan.
Description: Second edition. | San Francisco : Jossey-Bass, [2020] |
    Includes bibliographical references and index.
Identifiers: LCCN 2019040633 (print) | LCCN 2019040634 (ebook) | ISBN
    9781119595847 (hardback) | ISBN 9781119595786 (adobe pdf) | ISBN
    9781119595823 (epub)
Subjects: LCSH: Educational leadership. | School management and
    organization. | Educational change.
Classification: LCC LB2806 .F794 2020 (print) | LCC LB2806 (ebook) | DDC
    371.2—dc23
LC record available at https://lccn.loc.gov/2019040633
LC ebook record available at https://lccn.loc.gov/2019040634

Cover Design: Wiley
Cover Image: © Eoneren/iStock.com

Printed in the United States of America

HB Printing

V10015873_112719

Contents

To WLIW

Preface to the
Second Edition

WHAT IS A CULTURE OF CHANGE ANYWAY? I USE
the phrase in two ways. One is the fact that changes
are always rolling into and over all our organizations these
days. One form of leadership in this latter case is protecting
the organization from constant, superficial change. The second and more fundamental use is how to change the existing
culture so that it has the capacity to manage and incorporate
change on a continuous basis that serves the goals of the organization, including deliberately incorporating new goals and
their implementation.

The more complex society gets, the more sophisticated
leadership must become. Complexity means change, but
specifically it means rapidly occurring, unpredictable, nonlinear change. Moreover, the pace of change is ever increasing,
as James Gleick, the author of *Chaos*, pointed out in a book

called *Faster*, which he subtitled *The Acceleration of Just about Everything* (Gleick, 1999). That was two decades ago, much before the advent of the iPhone, introduced in 2007 and artificial intelligence! How do you lead in a culture such as ours, which seems to specialize in pell-mell innovation?

This is the leader's dilemma. On the one hand, failing to act when the environment around you is radically changing leads to extinction. On the other hand, making quick decisions under conditions of mind-racing mania can be equally fatal. Robert Steinberg said it best: "The essence of intelligence would seem to be in knowing when to think and act quickly, and knowing when to think and act slowly" (cited in Gleick, 1999, p. 114).

This book is about how leaders can focus on certain key change themes that will allow them to lead effectively under messy conditions. The book is also about how leaders foster leadership in others, thereby making themselves dispensable in the long run. And it is about how we can produce more "leaders of leaders."

Now 19 years after the first edition of "*Leading in a Culture of Change*" the five themes still hold true, but we have much more specificity about their role in change. And we need to relabel some of the concepts to make them more precise, relative to current knowledge. Moral purpose remains the rock, but we now focus on its actual impact and how to get it if you don't have it. Second, understanding change is laced with a new insight: *nuance*. In complex societies, effective change and nuance pretty much go hand in hand. Third, relationship building is still key but we have sorted out what effective and not-so-effective relationships are, which I examine under the banner of effective collaboration.

Fourth, knowledge building and sharing is ever critical, but now we see it in relation to "deep learning" that encompasses technology and innovation. Fifth, coherence making has turned out to be a powerful concept; we have pinpointed the role of leadership as coherence makers in complex times.

The other major development over the past 20 years is that the world has become much more complex, but more than that—the world is becoming ever more troubled. Worsening climate change, unknown job markets, greater superficial closeness via technology but less closeness, more stress and anxiety, and less trust decade by decade, and corresponding erosion of trust. All of this puts moral purpose to greater tests as it makes it more crucial. Leaders don't need to become better at a bad game; they need to change the game! The framework and examples I provide in this book will put leaders in a position to lead change under ever increasing challenges to help people and organizations thrive. Complexity always brings new opportunities but only when society has strong leadership dispersed across the system.

Schools and businesses increasingly have more in common because both are trying to find their way in ever challenging circumstances. In our own work over the past decade we have pretty much concluded that schools as we know them are past their due date. They no longer serve the purpose they were originally assigned some 200 years ago—to produce reliable workers for an industrial society. We are in the midst of trying to change that in our work on "deep learning" that we will take up in various parts of the book.

Clearly these are difficult, even threatening times—there is a lot going on. Not the least of these developments is the new realization that leadership is key to large-scale improvement yet must be radically different than it has been. Further, effective leadership is in very short supply. In the course of this book, I will map out the new leadership that will be required to take us forward from 2020 onward.

In complex, what I have called chaotic times, leaders must be able to operate under conditions that are not always clear—worse, not as clear as they appear to be. G.K. Chesterton identified the challenge best: "Life is not an illogicality, yet it is as trap for logicians . . . . Its exactitude is obvious, but its inexactitude hidden. Its wildness lies in wait" (quoted in Bernstein, 1996, p. 331). Coping with wildness lying in wait may not be a bad job description for leading in a culture of change.

One last point: Over the years, we have found that about 80% of our best ideas come from "leading practitioners." You will find that the ideas in this book are well grounded, and cutting edge. Thus, in the course of this book you will discover what it means to be leader in a culture of change. In many ways, the ideas and insights come from the horse's mouths, although I have been able to articulate it in precise and, I think, insightful language. Commit yourself to leading in a culture of change, and find out how in the following chapters.

Although there are overtones of saving the world in this book, the core message is: Make your organization the best it can be. To do this effectively, you have to take into account the bigger picture. This is a practical matter for me. You have "to go outside to become better inside," as we say. If many leaders do this, they will end up improving both the inside and the outside. All good solutions are system solutions.

Chapter One

Making Complexity Work

C HANGE IS A DOUBLE-EDGED SWORD. ITS RELENTLESS pace these days runs us off our feet. Yet when things are unsettled, we can find new ways to move ahead and to create breakthroughs not possible in stagnant societies. If you ask people to brainstorm words to describe change, they come up with a mixture of negative and positive terms. On the one side, fear, anxiety, loss, danger, panic, disaster; on the other, exhilaration, risk-taking, excitement, improvements, energizing. For better or for worse, change arouses emotions, and when emotions intensify, leadership is key.

Changing Culture

Changing culture—the focus of this book—is one of the hardest things that humankind faces. And if you don't change and adapt you become obsolete or extinct. Let's start with the father of the study of organizational culture, Edgar Schein (2010, 4th edition). Schein's formal definition of culture is:

> The culture of a group can be defined as a pattern of shared assumptions as it solves its problems of external adaptations and internal integration, which has worked well enough to be considered valid, and therefore to be taught to new members as the correct way to perceive, think, and feel in relation to those problems. (p. 18)

For example: "We protect each other against external criticism" would be one such example. Or "We share our best ideas with each other" would be another culture at work.

How do you know when it is time to change the culture? Some indicators would seem to be: Members are dissatisfied, disengaged, and stressed out. Or customers or clients look for alternatives to your institution. Apparently, it takes a great deal of unhappiness to take the steps to change. Some organizations or schools have been persistently unhappy but have taken little action to change the situation. Inertia seems to have a life of its own. Then when change is attempted, there appears to be many more ways to fail than to succeed. Schein says that one of the biggest mistakes that leaders make is to propose a "change in culture" without being clear or specific (p. 312). Leadership often gets the solution (and the way to go about it) wrong. When Dan Goleman (2000, pp. 82–83) studied leadership styles, he found two that had negative impact on the organization:

- Coercive—the leader demands compliance ("Do as I tell you").
- Pacesetter—sets high standards ("Do as I do, now").

With the coercive style, people resent and resist; with pace-setters, people get overwhelmed and burn out. Toxic cultures ensue and either the leader or large numbers of employees leave. The pacesetter seems positive but only at first. Goleman found:

> The leader [pacesetter] sets extremely high performance standards and exemplifies them her/himself. S/He is obsessive about doing things better and faster, and s/he asks the same of everyone around him. S/He quickly pinpoints poor performers and demands more from them. If they don't rise to the occasion, s/he replaces them with people who can. You would think such an approach would improve results, but it doesn't. In fact, the pacesetting style destroys climate. Many employees feel overwhelmed by the pacesetter's demands for excellence, and their morale drops—guidelines for working may be clear in the leader's head, but s/he does not state them clearly; s/he expects people to know what to do. (p. 86)

The pacesetter often ends up being a "Lone Ranger," as Superintendent Negroni from Springfield, Massachusetts, put it when he reflected on his experience (and on his eventual change to lead learner). During the first three years of Negroni's superintendency, his overall goal was "to change this inbred system":

> Intent on the ends, I operated as Lone Ranger. I didn't try to build relationships with the teachers' union or with the board. Instead, I worked around them. Most of the time, I felt that I was way out in front of them. I would change things on my own. (quoted in Senge et al., 2000, p. 426)

For all the changes he pushed through, Negroni says, "These were three brutal years for us. I was running so fast and making so many changes that I was getting tired. People around me were even more sick and tired" (pp. 426–427). Eventually, through reflective practice and feedback, Negroni moved to transforming the district into a "learning in-situation" proposition. Anticipating some of the themes we take up in subsequent chapters Negroni explains:

> Our most critical role at the central office is to support learning about learning, especially among principals—who will then do the same among teachers in their schools. At the beginning of the year, three or four central office administrators and I conducted forty-six school visits in forty-six days, with the principals of each school alongside us. Then the administrators and all forty-six principals met together to summarize what we had seen. This is one of a series of walk-throughs that principals do during the course of a school year—with me, with other central office administrators, and with each other. The sequence includes a monthly "grand round," when every principal in the district goes with me and the eight academic directors, to spend the day in one school. We break up into subgroups for hour-and-a-half visits, then come back and (still in subgroups) discuss what we saw. Then a representative from each subgroup makes a presentation to all of the principals. (quoted in Senge et al., 2000, p. 431)

So, this book is not about super leaders. Charismatic leaders inadvertently often do more harm than good because, at best, they provide episodic improvement followed by frustrated or despondent dependency. Superhuman leaders also do us another disservice: They are role models who can never be emulated. Deep and sustained reform depends on many of us, not just on the very few who appear to be extraordinary.

I need to define the nature and goal of this book, leading in a culture of change. It has two purposes. One is most organizations do not change, or at least do not change in time. My first goal is to get organizations to a point where their "change capacity" is at least at a level that meets Schein's basic definition: "deals with external adaptation and internal integration." This is everyday coping with the environment and corresponding integration. If organizations do this, that will indeed be engaged in steady change. Note that this definition does not mean that organizations take on whatever change comes along—that would be the pacesetter. There always needs to be selectivity to determine what is good for us and our clients according to our moral purpose (Chapter 2).

The second purpose is to get to the point where organizations proactively challenge the status quo. With all the challenges facing the world—and the world is increasingly troubled—we need greater proactivity about the future. Leaders in a culture of change cultivate a larger worldview.

I have never been fond of distinguishing between leadership and management. They overlap, and you need both qualities. But here is one difference that it makes sense to highlight: Leadership is needed for problems that do not have easy answers. The big problems of the day are complex, rife with paradoxes and dilemmas. For these problems there are no once-and-for-all answers. Yet we expect our leaders to provide solutions. We place leaders in untenable positions (or, alternatively, our system produces leaders who try to carry the day with populist, one-sided solutions that are as clear as they are oversimplified). Homer-Dixon (2000, p. 15) makes a similar observation:

> We demand that [leaders] solve, or at least manage, a multitude of interconnected problems that can develop into crises without warning; we require them to navigate an increasingly turbulent reality that is, in key aspects, literally incomprehensible to the human mind; we buffet them on every side with bolder, more powerful special interests that challenge every innovative policy idea; we sub-merge them in often unhelpful and distracting information; and we force them to decide and act at an ever faster pace.

Heifetz (1994) accuses us of looking for the wrong kind of leadership when the going gets tough:

> in a crisis … we call for someone with answers, decision, strength, and a map of the future, someone who knows where we ought to be going—in short someone who can make hard problems simple … Instead of looking for saviors, we should be calling for leadership that will challenge us to face problems for which there are no simple, painless solutions—problems that require us to learn new ways. (p. 21)

An alternative image of leadership, argues Heifetz (1994, p. 15), is one of "mobilizing people to tackle tough problems." Leadership, then, is not mobilizing others to solve problems we already know how to solve, but to help them confront problems that have never yet been successfully addressed. We will return to Heifetz (Heifetz & Linksky, 2017) in Chapter 7 when we delve deeper into leading complex change.

An Increasing Convergence

There is a remarkable convergence of ideas that *could* make leadership more effective in complex times (see Figure 1.1). First, a reality check: It is very hard to be as good a leader as the qualities in Figure 1.1 represent. Empirically, it seems that most leaders are less than competent. My view is that this is the case not because they are deficient as people but because it is so damn hard to be as good as needed (think for a moment about any 20 politicians you know).

Let's take Tomas Chamorrow-Premuzic (2019): "*Why so many incompetent men become leaders.*" He concludes that most leaders are incompetent, men more so. Let's see what and why.

Chamorrow-Premuzic first presents various statistics: 75% of people quit their jobs because of their direct line manager; in a very large survey, human resource managers rated only 26% of their current leaders positively; 70% of employees are not engaged at work; and so on. The main point here is not that women do better (they do, but there are not many of them), but that most leaders do not have positive impacts. The biggest culprit is (over) confidence. It seems that the majority of current leaders project strong confidence both before and after they are appointed.

Statistically, confidence bears little relationship to competence. There is little overlap between how smart people think they are and how smart they actually are. At the end of the day, too many leaders (and most are men) are more confident about their leadership than their actual competence warrants.

The flip side of this argument is compatible with where we are going in this book: "the most competent people will exhibit much self-criticism and self-doubt, especially relative to their expertise" (Chamorrow-Premuzic, 2019, p. 24). Or, "expertise increases self-knowledge which includes self-awareness of one's limitations" (p. 24). We will see later that humility with courage and a relentless drive to solve important problems is the most powerful combination.

In the meantime, my start-up message is that most leaders are not highly competent. When it comes to effective leadership, you can't judge a book by its cover; and leading in a culture of change involves qualities that are below the surface, and not so much the obvious ones of confidence, presence, and articulation.

By contrast, there is, I will argue, a remarkable convergence of theories, knowledge bases, ideas, and strategies that help us confront complex problems that do not have easy answers. This convergence creates a new mind-set—a framework for thinking about and leading complex change more powerfully than ever before. This convergence is even stronger in the present that it was almost two decades ago when we published the first edition. Figure 1.1 summarizes the framework as updated.

Chapters 2 through 6 are devoted to building the case for the powerful knowledge base represented by these five components of effective leadership. Briefly, *moral purpose* means acting with the intention of making a positive difference in the lives of employees, customers, and society as a whole. This is

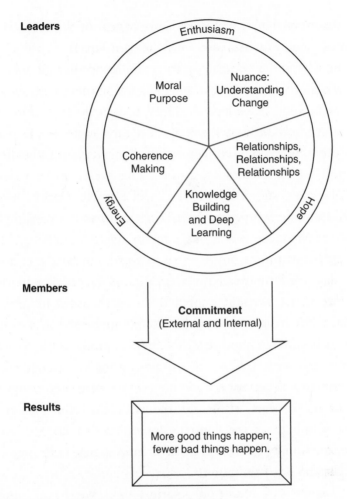

Figure 1.1. A framework for leadership.

an obvious value with which many of us can identify, but I will argue in Chapter 2 that there may be inevitable evolutionary reasons why moral purpose will become more and more prominent and that, in any case, to be effective in complex times, leaders must be guided by moral purpose. We will take up case studies from both business and education that will demonstrate that moral purpose is critical to the long-term success of all organizations, and the world itself.

In Chapter 3, I turn to the complex matter of *understanding the dynamics of change*. Moral purpose without an understanding of change will lead to moral martyrdom as passion gets dashed on the rocks of reality. Moreover, leaders who combine a commitment to moral purpose with a healthy respect for the complexities of the change process not only will be more successful but also will unearth deeper moral purpose. Understanding the change process is exceedingly elusive. Management books contain reams of advice, but the advice is often contradictory, general, and at the end of the day confusing and nonactionable. I mentioned in the preface that I have long concluded that the most insightful ideas come from leading practitioners immersed in sorting out successful from unsuccessful change. I have worked with many such leaders. Chapter 3 draws on the knowledge base of effective practitioners by identifying nine key insights about the concept of change that will give you a greater understanding of the human dimensions of change and correspondingly will enable you to lead change with greater insight and less frustration.

Chapter 4 focuses on relationships. We have found that the single factor common to every successful change initiative is that *relationships* improve. More specifically, collaboration with others—teamwork that has certain precise qualities—is what counts. If relationships improve, things get better. If they remain the same or get worse, ground is lost. Thus, leaders must be consummate relationship builders with diverse people and groups—especially with people different from themselves. Effective leaders constantly foster purposeful interaction and problem solving, and are wary of easy consensus.

Relationship as an end in itself is not the point; focused collaboration in relation to the work is key. We are learning that this work must be precise in relation to the goals, and that precision is a developmental process. This leads to valuable insights such as "Strive for precision, but avoid prescription"—the latter being the death knell for positive change. We have also identified new ideas about effective group work. For example, autonomy and collaboration can and must coexist. Once you get inside the change process you uncover powerful subtleties. This is why I titled my newest book *Nuance*. The best change ideas are beneath the surface but they are accessible, and once grasped make a world of difference.

In Chapter 5, I examine our new work on *deep learning* that engages students or employees in the pursuit of knowledge and problem-solving. The ideas examined are highly congruent with the previous three themes. We live, after all, in the knowledge society, but that term is a cliché. What is most revealing is that new theoretical and empirical studies of successful organizations unpack the operational meaning of the general term *knowledge organization*. I will show how leaders commit themselves to constantly generating and increasing knowledge inside and outside the organization. What has been discovered is that, first, people will not voluntarily share knowledge unless they feel some moral commitment to do so; second, people will not share unless the dynamics of change favor exchange; and, third, that data without relationships merely cause more information glut. Put another way, turning information into knowledge is a *social* process. We will also take up new developments involving deep learning—schools that promise to transform, or, if you like, set out to save that moribund institution we call school. We will see that we need a new conception of learning, greater and bigger moral purpose, an understanding of the change process, and teamwork if we are to create and share knowledge.

Chapter 6 takes up our new work on the vital concept of "coherence making." Business leaders and gurus have spent eons trying to align organizations to goals, visions, strategic plans, assessments, and the like. Mintzberg (2004) in a devastating critique dismisses most traditional leadership programs as dealing with abstractions or other de-contextualized problems. *Leadership for change* takes us inside context. It is not strategic alignment—a rational concept—that counts but rather, coherence—a subjective, emotional phenomenon. Effective leaders enable daily coherence making.

In the final chapter, "Leadership for Change," I double back and ask, what are the essential qualities of effective leaders who operate in increasingly complex times, and then importantly, how do we develop such leaders on a continuous basis? I show that the moral purpose of work, life, and even survival itself is increasingly at stake.

There is another set of seemingly more personal characteristics that all effective leaders possess, which I have labeled the *energy-courage-relentlessness* constellation. I do not think it is worth debating whether this constellation is a cause or an effect of the five leadership components. No doubt there is a dynamic, reciprocal relationship between the two sets. Energetic-courageous-relentless-leaders can "cause" greater moral purpose in themselves, tackle change head on, naturally build relationships and knowledge, and seek coherence to consolidate moral purpose.

But the flip side also occurs: By effectively leading in a culture of change, leaders also develop greater courage (in themselves and others) to do even more. We will encounter leaders immersed in the five aspects of leadership who can't help feeling and acting more energetic, and relentless. As we will see, the most effective leaders *become* more courageous as a result of their experiences. Yet they retain their humility and empathy for others. The notion that courage becomes stronger and more evident as leaders develop is a powerful insight and phenomenon.

Whatever the case, effective leaders make people feel that even the most difficult problems can be tackled productively. They are always hopeful—conveying a sense of optimism and an attitude of never giving up in the pursuit of highly valued goals. Their enthusiasm and confidence (not certainty) are, in a word, infectious; such leaders become more trusted and attract greater commitment—provided that they incorporate all five leadership capacities in their day-to-day behavior.

Note also how the five capacities together operate in a checks and balances fashion. Leaders with deep moral purpose provide guidance, but they can also have blinders if ideas are not challenged through the dynamics of change, the give and take of relationships, and the ideas generated by new knowledge. Similarly, coherence is seen as part and parcel of complexity and can never be completely achieved (newcomers come and go; new challenges appear, and so on). Leaders in a culture of change value and see as valuable the tensions inherent in addressing hard-to-solve problems, because that is where the greatest accomplishments lie.

Figure 1.1 also shows how leaders who are steeped in the five core capacities by definition evince and generate long-term commitment in those with whom they work. Effective leaders, because they live and breathe the five aspects of leadership, find themselves committed to stay the course (in a sense, they are also inspired by others in the organization as they interact around moral purposes, new knowledge, and the achievement of periodic coherence). And, of course, they mobilize more and more people to become willing to tackle tough problems. We have to be careful when we talk about commitment. In the past, we have written about blind commitment or groupthink—when the group goes along uncritically with the leader or the group (Fullan & Hargreaves, 1992). Leaders can be powerful, and so can groups, which means they can be powerfully wrong. This is why the five dimensions of leadership must work in concert. They provide a check against uninformed commitment.

Even when commitment is evidently generated, there are qualifiers. Argyris (2000, p. 40) has helped us make the crucial distinction between *external* and *internal* commitment:

> These differ in how they are activated and in the source of energy they utilize. External commitment is triggered by management policies and practices that enable employees to accomplish their tasks. Internal commitment derives from energies internal to human beings that are activated because getting a job done is intrinsically rewarding.

Argyris notes that "when someone else defines objectives, goals, and the steps to be taken to reach them, whatever commitment exists will be external" (p. 41).

Moral purpose is usually accompanied by a sense of urgency. Leaders in some such cases are in a hurry. If they are in too much of a hurry, they will fail—you can't bulldoze change. If leaders are more sophisticated, they may set up a system of pressure and support, which in the short run will obtain noticeable desired results, but these will mainly be derived from external commitment. They are unlikely to have any lasting value.

At this stage of the discussion, we need only make one additional point: What about outcomes? The litmus test of all leadership is whether it mobilizes people's commitment to putting their energy into actions designed to improve things. It is individual commitment, but it is above all collective mobilization. Generating internal over external commitment is the mark of effective leadership.

What are the outcomes of all this effective leadership and commitment? In Figure 1.1, I have deliberately referred to results very generally as causing "more good things to happen" and "fewer bad things to happen." I will be presenting case studies from both business and education that provide the specifics of impact. In the case of business, good things are economic viability, customer satisfaction, employee pride, and a sense of being valuable to society. In schools, good things are enhanced student performance, increased capacity of teachers, greater involvement of parents and community members, engagement of students, all-around satisfaction and enthusiasm about going further, and greater pride for all in the system. More than this, in our latest work on deep learning we find in students a greater sense of wanting to make a difference in society, immediately and in the long run. We captured this in the phrase—indeed in the finding—that students innately want to "engage the world; change the world" through their learning and development.

In both cases—business and education—the reduction of bad things means fewer aborted change efforts; less demoralization of employees; fewer examples of piecemeal, uncoordinated reform; and a lot less wasted effort and resources.

This book delves into the complexities of leadership evidenced in Figure 1.1. It is about making complexity work though five synergistic themes. It provides insights, strategies, and, ultimately, better theories of knowledge and action suited to leadership in complex times. In the final chapter we will examine more directly the question of how new leaders can be developed. How to become more effective as a leader is of growing concern for all those in positions to make a difference; how to foster large numbers of leaders in all areas of society is a system question more worrisome today than ever before. If leadership does not become more attractive, doable, and exciting, public and private institutions will deteriorate. If the experience of rank-and-file members of the organization does not improve, there will not be a pool of potential leaders to cultivate—a classic chicken-and-egg problem. Good leaders foster good leadership at other levels. Leadership at other levels produces a steady stream of future leaders for the system as a whole. Bad or ineffective leaders do the opposite—they make matters worse in a downward spiral.

I also have to say that humans face one enormous obstacle that no other beings face, namely *learning anxiety*— specifically, anxiety when it comes to learning something new. Schein (p. 104) identifies five possible/probable learning anxieties in the face of change:

1. Fear of loss of power or position

2. Fear of temporary [or worse] incompetence

3. Fear of punishment for incompetence

4. Fear of loss of personal identity

5. Fear of loss of group membership

The odds favor the status quo—and if they do that, they favor *decline*. In dynamic times, there is no such thing as standing still. When people contemplate change, what is being lost is palpable and immediate; the gains are theoretical and in the future. How many people do you know where the persistence of the current situation is bad for the person, and is obvious to everyone? Yet they do not entertain change. If you add to that the fact that you can't trust most leaders to get it right, the odds of positive change dwindle.

Leading in a culture of change is for leaders who want to beat the odds. Such leaders are not fearless; they see anxiety as a normal part of significant change. This book is for leaders who want to increase their knowledge and skill in dealing with the human and social factors that lay at the bottom of bad or good change. If this prospect instills fear in you as a future leader, you have made the first right step. The rest of the book shows you what else you will need to know.

Leaders will increase their effectiveness if they continually work on the five components of leadership—if they pursue moral purpose, understand the change process, develop grounded collaboration, foster deep knowledge building, and strive for coherence—with energy, courage, and relentlessness, and a share of doubt and anxiety. The culture of change beckons.

Chapter Two

Moral Purpose

Y OU DON'T HAVE TO BE MOTHER TERESA TO HAVE moral purpose. Some people are deeply passionate about improving life (sometimes to a fault, if they lack one or more of the other four components of leadership: understanding of the change process, strong team developers, deep knowledge building, and coherence making among multiple priorities). Others have a more cognitive approach, displaying less emotion but still being intensely committed to betterment. Whatever one's style, every leader, to be effective, must have and work on improving his or her moral purpose.

Defining Moral Purpose

Moral purpose is about both ends and means. In education, an important end is to make a difference in the lives of students. But the means of getting to that end are also crucial.

If you don't treat others (e.g., teachers) well and fairly, you will be a leader without followers (see Chapter 4, in which I describe how effective leaders constantly work on developing relationships at all levels of the organization). Of course, a case can be made that leading with integrity is not just instrumental. To strive to improve the quality of how we live together is a moral purpose of the highest order. Sergiovanni (1999, p. 17) draws the same conclusion about what he calls the lifeworld of leadership:

> Ask the next five people you meet to list three persons they know, either personally or from history, who they consider to be authentic leaders. Then have them describe these leaders. Chances are your respondents will mention integrity, reliability, moral excellence, a sense of purpose, firmness of conviction, steadiness, and unique qualities of style and substance that differentiate the leaders they choose from others. Key in this list of characteristics is the importance of substance, distinctive qualities, and moral underpinnings. Authentic leaders anchor their practice in ideas, values, and commitments, exhibit distinctive qualities of style and substance, and can be trusted to be morally diligent in advancing the enterprises they lead. Authentic leaders, in other words, display character, and character is the defining characteristic of authentic leadership.

At the loftiest level, moral purpose is about how humans evolve over time, especially in relation to how they relate to each other. Ridley (1996) and Sober and Wilson (1998) trace the evolution of self-centered and cooperative behavior in animals, insects, and humans. What makes humans different, says Ridley, is culture. Ideas, knowledge, practices and beliefs, and the like enter consciousness and can be passed on "by direct infection from one person to another" (p. 179). Ridley raises the interesting evolutionary hypothesis that "cooperative groups thrive and selfish ones do not, so cooperative societies have survived at the expense of others" (p. 175). Thus, leaders in all organizations, whether they know it or not, contribute for better or for worse to moral purpose in their own organizations and in society as a whole. However, as society overall becomes more impersonal, we may be witnessing a combination of greater closeness within local groups, along with greater distance between groups that are distal and unknown—a point I take up in Chapter 7.

Sober and Wilson (1998) state that it is futile to argue whether people are driven by egoistic (self-centered) or altru-istic (unselfish) motives. The fact is that all effective leaders—most people, actually—are driven by both. Sober and Wilson call this "motivational pluralism [which] is the view that we have both egoistic and altruistic ultimate desires" (p. 308). This is why everyday leaders shouldn't expect to be like Mother Theresa. (And who knows, maybe she got a lot of pleasure out of helping others.) Most of us have mixed motives, and that is perfectly fine.

I will also show that moral purpose doesn't stand alone. We will see that leaders who work on the five qualities in this book—not just the obvious first quality, which is moral purpose itself, but all five components in concert—will, by definition, find themselves steeped in moral purpose. Whether you are an insurance executive or a school principal, you simply cannot be effective without behaving in a morally purposeful way. And if you follow the lessons in this book, you won't have to *plan* to be more moral in your pursuit; it will come naturally. Moral purpose is profoundly built into the five components of leadership as they are carried out in practice. The complexity of pursuing moral purpose in a culture of change can be best illustrated through case examples. I select cases equally from education and from business to show that the issues of leadership are increasingly common across both types of organizations.

The Case for Moral Purpose

Is moral purpose among humans guaranteed because it is built into our evolutionary genes? I used to think that was the case. Evolutionary forces seemed to take their course for much of the past 10,000 years (the time period where we have some knowledge that humans have existed on a scale living in groups around the world). Broadly speaking, each generation seems to be better off than the previous one (until the present, most of us were better off than our parents). Now I am not so sure. It could go either way. Why? Because humans are intervening by deliberately, but not always beneficially, attempting to shape the future. "Leading in a culture of change" takes the position, "Why take a chance?" Leaders who embody the five qualities of leading in a culture of change help shape the future for the better.

Let's examine these questions: What is the state of moral leadership in business and in education? How moral purpose connects to success in a way that no other force can? And how is the *content* of moral purpose changing in education in this very period?

Moral Purpose in Business and Education

LRN (2019) tracks "the State of Moral Leadership in business." LRN defines moral leadership as "how leaders touch hearts, not just minds—how they enlist others in a shared and significant endeavor and create the conditions where everyone can contribute their fullest talent and realize their deepest humanity" (p. 3). Here are the main findings:

1. 87% of respondents say that the need for moral leadership is greater than ever.

2. 94% of managers and executives who lead with moral authority, rather than relying on the formal authority of their roles, are considered effective in achieving business goals. Moral leaders are also regarded as more effective at encouraging innovation (90% vs. 11%).

3. Only 7% said their managers consistently exhibit the behaviors of moral leadership; 59% say their managers exhibit few or none of the behaviors of moral leadership.

4. The researchers identified seven practices that employees see moral leaders doing. They start with a cause, see employees as people, foster freedom, demonstrate humility, act with courage, seek the truth, and uphold ethical standards. (Reader: Compare these traits with those of effective leaders that I identify throughout this book and summarize in Chapter 7.)

The survey found that "90% of the people who work for moral leaders say they feel seen, heard, and respected; 89%

say they feel like they matter, and 95% say they are inspired to contribute their best efforts when they work for these leaders" (pp. 4–8).

The bottom line is that LRN found that moral leadership is consistently good for business, *and is in short supply* (only 14% of leaders consistently demonstrate most of the moral leadership behaviors).

LRN authors then identify four pillars of moral leadership: let purpose lead; inspire and elevate others; be animated by values and virtues; and keep building "moral muscle" (not the best phrase in my view, but which means constantly attending to moral purpose).

The obvious conclusion is that moral purpose is *good for business and good for life*. Put in terms of "leading in a culture of change," all five components in our model as a set constitute full-blown moral purpose in action.

In education, one would think that moral purpose would fare better than in business. After all, education of the young is a moral undertaking. I would have to say that by the criteria *of moral purpose accomplished* (i.e., that the majority of students do well at school and as human beings), education falls far short. This is not a blame statement. It is damn tough to serve all students, given the diversity and circumstances of starting points. What we have instead is that the majority of school districts have moral purpose in their vision statements and strategic plans, but the track record of accomplishments is substantially wanting. I titled one of my books *Moral Imperative Realized* (Fullan, 2011). When one looks closely, you can find examples of success (schools going from low to high performance), but they are decidedly in the minority. In a moment, we will look at one of these exceptions. My point will be that it can be done, but will require the mobilization of the power of our full model and its five components.

As we turn to an example, let us consider the hypothetical question to a large group of teachers: "Can all students learn?" Most of us would predict that teachers would say yes. And they would mean it. However, if some of these teachers were in a school where many students were not in fact learning year after year, I would doubt that deep down they would believe that all students could learn. What could change their minds?

I can tell you two things that won't change their minds. One is "research evidence." Here is a school just like yours—similar demographics and resources—that is highly successful. A second approach that will not work is what I call "increased moral exhortation." The leader states the moral imperative in a louder voice and more frequently. The first approach (research evidence) tells you it can be done, while the second (moral exhortation) says it should be done. Neither tells you *how* it can be accomplished. And the *how* perspective is also tricky; people don't get it if you tell them the step-by-step means of making a change.

What, then, could be done to successfully challenge the status quo? The type of thing that does work is giving people new experiences in relatively nonthreatening circumstances with help from peers or others that results in giving students opportunity to be successful where they are indeed learning—easy to say, hard to do. In fact, the hard-to-do consists of the orchestration of the five components of the model that guides this books: moral purpose, understanding change, collaboration, deep learning, and coherence making—all with diverse people.

Let's illustrate with a tough example (other cases will be presented in subsequent chapters). In my book *Nuance,* I report on the case of Benjamin Adlard Primary School—a high-poverty primary school in Lincolnshire, England, that, to say the least, was a toxic mess and had been for at least a decade. At the time, Marie-Claire Bretherton was a successful principal of another high-poverty school in the same broad Lincolnshire area. Her assignment was to turn the school around, removing it from what England calls "special measures"—a status that the school had had for several years.

Benjamin Adlard has about 30 staff with 220 pupils. Nearly 70% of the students are on free school meals. The school population is highly transient, with 33% coming and going in a given year; 30% are in special needs. Marie-Claire sized up the initial situation:

> I know what I am doing in my own school that works, but I knew it was not going to translate into Benjamin Adlard. The context was different, the staff was different, and although the mission and the values were the same, the approach needed to be different. I could have taken the outstanding curriculum model in my own school and imposed it, or transferred some great teachers from my school to teach there. But I knew intuitively that this wouldn't work. I knew that as soon as I brought someone in and said here is an expert who is going to come and solve your problems that I would immediately undermine any sense of them owning the improvement journey, and their ability to learn. (interview, June 2018)

Bretherton continued:

I interviewed every single member of staff from cleaner to deputy head, just asking them everything they could tell me about the school and its history. They said to me whatever you think you know it is not going to work here; we've tried everything. These children just aren't capable of succeeding in school; the challenges they face in life are just too big … At my first staff meeting I said you may think I am going to sack you all. That's not what I am going to do. All I ask is that you turn up every day and that you are willing to learn, and that's all I need from you. We'll do it together. That was very countercultural and a big gamble. You know we didn't lose anybody. All of them stayed. (Interview, June 2018)

There are a lot of details in the Adlard case about establishing trust, skilling-up the workforce, managing students, and giving and receiving help that I won't go into here (see Fullan, 2019, pp. 32–42). Instead, let's get inside the thinking of the leader.

When I asked Bretherton what she had learned about leadership, she responded:

I think I have probably underestimated in the past the power of your own sense of vision and hope, and your own mental discipline … Just being able to conjure up in yourself optimism and hope where you are in the face of somebody who tells you that it is not possible. What I learned is about the leadership of humanity.

Later in the interview, Bretherton reflected on why she took the job.

> I visited the school. The playground was a wasteland of concrete. The pupils were pale; some looked malnourished and unhappy. The acting headteacher had no hope that things could ever be any better. She had lost faith in the system. The stories of the children included backgrounds of child prostitution, trafficking, domestic abuse, parental drug abuse and alcoholism, child brutality, child pornography. None of these children were older than 9 years of age.
>
> The thing that broke my heart was not just that bad things had happened to these children, but it was that the staff had no aspirations, no vision, and no hope. (Interview 2018)

Two years later, the school was off special measures and won an award for being "School of the year: Making a difference." The school is now oversubscribed, with students/parents and staff alike wanting to come and be there.

The Pervasive Power of Moral Purpose

As the world gets more complex and as the questions of our planet's mortality loom larger and more evident, the link between the moral purpose of our institutions and our own individual well-being becomes more intertwined. In addressing the situation, we have a leadership problem and an employee problem.

Gallup (Clifton & Harter, 2019) just completed a massive compilation of more than 30 years of studies of workplace tracking. Gallup's main finding was that "the single biggest factor in your organization's long-term success is the quality of managers and team leaders" (p. 12).

The bad news, as we will see in a moment, is the very low level of employee engagement in most companies. The good news is that the fate of organizations, and the fate of employees, are fundamentally connected. Incremental increases in this connection would yield huge dividends for organizations, employees, and their clients. One of the advantages of starting at a low bar is that initial success may be possible, and may have a leverage effect, given its mutual desirability.

We can start with the existing situation. Gallup finds there is a growing awareness and interest on the part of the young in their own and others' *human potential*. Most millennials (born between 1980 and 1996), and Generation Z (born 1997 and later) are increasingly interested in doing something worthwhile, including having a worthwhile job. These are the six biggest changes in the past 20 years that Gallup found:

1. Millennials and Generation Z don't just work for a paycheck—they want a purpose. They want to work for organizations that have a purpose and mission.

2. Millennials and Generation Z are no longer pursuing job satisfaction [in the narrow sense]; they want development.

3. [They] don't want bosses; they want coaches.

4. [They] don't want annual reviews; they want engaging conversations.

5. [They] don't want managers that fixate on their weaknesses; they want to develop strengths.

6. It's not my job—it's my life. (pp. 17–18)

Gallup then notes a major discrepancy between old-fashioned management and the new set of expectations. The practice of management, Gallup concludes, has been stuck in time for more than 30 years. Gallup found that only 15% of workers are engaged in work (p. 11), and that 70% of the variance in team engagement is determined solely by the manager.

Gallup proceeds with an analysis of problems and solutions that are essentially congruent with the chapters in *Leading in a Culture of Change*. Just about every solution looks like developing purposeful partnerships between managers and employees. For new hires, the conversation should be around questions such as:

"What do we believe around here?" "What are my strengths?," "What is my role?," "Who are my partners?," and "What does my future here look like?"

Gallup's list of seven expectations for success—*because they are, in essence, built on the notion of a culture of change*—end up pretty much what you will see in the pages of this book: build relationships, develop people, lead change, inspire others, think critically, communicate clearly, and create accountability (Clifton & Harter, 2019, p. 63).

If we turn to education, we have a surprisingly similar story. I say *surprisingly* because education of all fields should have moral purpose handed to them on a plate. What could be higher purpose than educating the next generation of citizens? Yet 30–50% of teachers leave teaching in the first five years (how about the one teacher who said, "I felt like the soldier dropped behind enemy lines with nothing more than orders," Niver, 2013). Or the drop in teacher satisfaction from 62% who reported feeling "very satisfied" in 2008 to 32% in 2013 (Metropolitan Life Insurance 2013). Even worse, only 33% of teachers reported being "actively engaged," along with 13% who were "actively disengaged" (they had completely opted out). In all cases, business or education, the majority of employees are not happy or productive.

I am an optimist, and I read the social tea leaves, when I say that the above dismal figures for both business and education are at the end of a very bad period (i.e., there are signs that I will spell out in this book that we are at a critical juncture in the history of humankind that indicate that dramatic changes will occur in the next decade). The factors and dynamics are so powerful that the outcome could go either way. Hence, we need the forces and insights of "leading in a culture of change."

Questionable developments in education from 1990 to 2010 consisted of what I have called "wrong policy drivers" (drivers are policies; wrong drivers are policies that don't work), I identified four major wrong drivers: negative accountability, individualism, technology, and an overload of ad hoc initiatives (Fullan, 2011). Negative accountability focused on standardized tests and punitive outcomes, and strangely offered very little help to get better. Performance stagnated or worsened. Individualism is more subtle. It involves seeking the solution through investments in human capital. If only we could get better teachers, and better principals. Not a bad idea as part of the solution, but as a standalone strategy—that is, without addressing the role of school cultures—the system will eat up individuals faster than you can produce them. Pretty soon, you have the syndrome that I refer to later as, "How are we going to keep them down on the farm once they've seen the farm?" If the farm looks that bad, people will stop coming to it—in fact, they will leave. At the same time, technology runs rampant. If you don't have a plan, technology has its random way, adding up to no net gain. In fact, the negative consequences seem to be reaching dangerous accelerating levels (see Newport's 2019 *Digital Minimalism* and Williams (2019 *Stand out of our light*)). The fourth wrong driver was the proliferation of ad hoc policies that made it increasingly difficult to recognize whether there was *any* "system" at all at work.

The four wrong policy drivers stagnated development or made matters worse as more and more educators became alienated and gave up. Now, almost a decade after the publication of the wrong drivers, more and more people at all levels of the system seem to be agreeing that there is indeed something wrong with the policies we have been pursuing. I can't say that people saw the light in a flash; it is more likely that a combination of circumstances began to show cracks in the system (one is reminded of the Canadian poet and singer Leonard Cohen's anthem: "There is a crack in everything; that's how the light gets in"). It almost makes one believe in evolution to consider why and how the Millennials and Generation Z represent changing in directions more congruent with the new approaches that are represented in this book.

No matter; the conditions are becoming more favorable for a new convergence between the values and interests of management and employees, and between educators and students. Two factors account for the change: one has a small impact, and the other has potentially a revolutionary role to play. Relative to the former—the slow boat of more knowledge about better management—has helped. Still, inertia often prevails. To activate the latent positive forces, we need leaders who act and develop in others the traits that are embedded in Figure 1.1.

Since the publication of the first edition of *Leading in a Culture of Change* (Fullan 2001), we are seeing a growing number of positive examples that support the framework embodied in Figure 1.1. Sisodia, Wolfe, and Sheth (2007) completed an in-depth study of what they called "firms of endearment" (FoE). The authors report that in one large-scale study, only 13.8% of respondents said that their organization had an "enthusiastic workforce." They then set out to find exceptions. Sisodia et al. began their search for FoEs by identifying companies that met their humanistic performance criterion—firms that paid equal attention to all five stakeholders (customers, employees, investors, partners, society). They proceeded in several steps to verify the list, ending with 28 companies ranging alphabetically from Amazon to Whole Foods (Toyota was on the list, for example).

Sisodia and colleagues then conducted an analysis of the financial success of the companies over a 10-year period (1996–2006) using the S&P performance index. Here is what they found: "*The public FOEs returned 1,026 percent for investors ... compared to 122 percent for S&Ps 500; that's more than an 8-to-1 ratio!"* (Sisodia, Wolfe, & Sheth, 2007, p. iv; italics in original).

In-depth studies by other researchers confirm these findings. Gittell's (2003) study of Southwest Airlines is a clear example. With all the ups and downs in the airline industry—fuel costs, 9/11, competition—Southwest has had multiple decades of profit without ever laying off employees. On all measures—costs per seat mile, aircraft productivity (hours in use), and labor productivity—Southwest consistently outperforms the competition. Gittel concludes the Southwest's "secret ingredient" is "its ability to build and sustain high-performance relationships among managers, employees, unions, and suppliers" (p. xi).

A study of Canada's best-managed companies identified similar themes associated with success (Grank, Hughes, & Hunter, 2006). From Magnatta Winery to Cirque du Soleil, the success of these companies is predicated on attracting and investing in high-performing employees who provide superior service through innovation and commitment to their peers, to customers, and to the companies themselves.

Need more convincing? Not to be outdone by Gallup, Google conducted its own longitudinal study of team performance in what it labeled "Project Aristotle" (in honor of his observation that "the whole is greater than the sum of its parts"). Massive analysis later, Google found that it was not the quality of individuals that mattered but, rather, the nature of the team. In particular, Google found five interrelated qualities associated with success:

1. *Psychological safety.* Team members feel safe to take risks and be vulnerable in front of each other.

2. *Dependability*. Team members get things done on time and meet Google's high bar for excellence.

3. *Structure and clarity*. Team members have clear roles, plans, and goals.

4. *Meaning*. Work is personally important to team members.

5. *Impact*. Team members think their work matters and creates change. (Google, 2019, p. 6)

Google's advice for leaders correspondingly follows (Google, 2019):

- Frame the work as a learning problem, not an execution problem.

- Acknowledge your own fallibility.

- Model curiosity—ask lot of questions.

I hope the reader realizes that these findings are pretty much what I been talking about in this book—*they confirm some of the essential content in Leading in a Culture of Change!*

I referred to this phenomenon of high-performance companies that seemed to benefit their employees, their workers, and investors as the "slow-boat" route to progress. Here's why. As far as I can tell, the proportion of companies like this does not seem to be on the increase. Second, many—I would say the majority—of the high performers eventually fall from the list. Overall, the rate of departures from the list at best was matched by new additions, not by an increase in overall numbers. Slow boat indeed! We can only conclude two things: that what works is increasingly clear and consistent across studies and practice, and that given the clarity and limited spread of these ideas and practices, *sustaining these practices must be very hard to do*. That is why we need new leadership at all levels (see Chapter 7).

The Promise of Fast Boats

We have the crystal-clear knowledge of the FoE, and Gallup, and Google. As I noted, the list of effective companies has not grown. Some companies still benefit investors and management more than employees, although their success will likely not last, given our analysis. And technology is disruptive, likely with net negative implications for employees, at least in the short run.

Has anything changed that might reverse the negative trend or state? Hopefully, the knowledge of new modes of organizational learning that I am featuring in this chapter will help. More promising, I think, is that we see in young people in society at large, and in schools, a different and growing breed. They have better values (see the Gallup six core values cited above); they are less likely to accept a bad status quo. They are more ready to do something about it (see Fullan, Quinn & McEachen, 2018; Fullan, Gardner, & Drummy, 2019, and Chapter 5 on "Knowledge Building and Deep Learning").

The danger of the world not surviving and the increasing moral purpose of young people are heading for a showdown—*therein lies the fast boat*. The moral purpose and knowledge of successful organizations that I have just reviewed, combined with the moral purpose of employees and students (that we already know spills over into societal concerns in both cases), can be the deep salvation that we need.

The first of my *Six Secrets of Change* (Fullan, 2008) was "Love your employees." In effect, I said: "If you want to love your employees, create the conditions in which they can succeed." In essence, it is part and parcel of the fast boat. One foundation of leading in a culture of change is to secure the moral purpose of your organization or entity as consisting of the integrated efforts of leaders, employee/students, and their interface with society. For the first time ever, I would say the conditions are possible (I dare not say favorable) to transform some of our key institutions—businesses and schools—as part of transforming societies. I wish I could say that governments are just as likely to lead this effort, but nothing in this century indicates that this is likely to happen. It will take sustained pressure from the bottom and the middle. This upward pressure is an essential part of *leading in a culture of change,* as we will see in subsequent chapters (see, especially, Chapter 6, "Coherence Making").

Conclusion

There is a lot more to moral purpose than moral purpose. It is not a state; it is a dynamic process. Moral purpose to be effective must embody all five elements of our change model depicted in Figure 1.1. Moral purpose, to be effective, should be pursued in its own right, but especially through the dynamics of successful change, purposeful collaboration, deep knowledge, and coherence making.

In the 2001 edition, I concluded that moral purpose was getting stronger, and that evolution favored its continued development and eventual dominance. Now I am not so sure. We have lost ground on moral purpose since 2001. The world is more troubled in ever-scary ways, which I think is causing moral leadership to come to the fore, especially among young people but linked to sympatico adults. The LRN research comments on this phenomenon.

> One of the important trends we see in the private sector is an increasing number of top leaders taking strong moral stands on social and political issues—immigration, for example. We believe this is reflects the blurring of the lines between public and private spheres in an interconnected world and an acknowledgement that customers, employees, and other stakeholders expect corporations to take moral stands. (p. 11)

In education, the main moral issue is that inequity of student achievement is increasingly on the rise, and that the narrow achievement agenda is making matters worse with inequity increasing, along with stress and anxiety of students at all socioeconomic status (SES) levels. We used to think that society self-corrects and even that evolution favors such a correction (cooperative societies prevail). For the first time, prominent neuroscientists are questioning the inevitability of goodness.

Antonio Damasio (2018), the great cognitive neuroscientist, shows that over the past 10,000 years, humankind could always rely on the brain to adapt, connect with others, and arrive at ever-higher levels of functioning. David Sloan Wilson (2019), the evolutionary biologist, is beginning to have doubts. Evolutionary forces under the right conditions (e.g., where cooperation wins out over competition) can function in a positive sense to confirm and extend our collective future. Up to the present, much of evolution has been genetically shaped (i.e., in the absence of conscious choices). At the present, cultural forces created by humankind have joined evolutionary genetics as potential drivers of change. The actions of our cultures include impacts on climate, trust in society, and the unknown impact of artificial intelligence.

David Sloan Wilson summarizes this phenomenon in what can only be interpreted as ominous words:

> The products of cultural evolution... adapt human populations to their environments much faster than genetic evolution—at times benefitting me at your expense, us at their expense, or all of us at he expense of future generations. To overcome these limitations, we must carefully direct the process of cultural evolution toward planetary sustainability. (p. 111)

I hope that readers can detect where this is taking us. In the past, we didn't have to worry as much about where the planet, including society, was taking us. It always worked out! Today, it is obvious that the actions of myriad individuals and groups have produced powerful societal forces beyond our individual control. It is also obvious that some of the developments are soul and planet destroying. I have to believe that both genetic and cultural evolution favor the rise of moral leaders in the sense that I have used it in this chapter. It is not guaranteed, but it is probable. In any case, business and education leaders in the future will need to step out more and more into society concerned with the evolving state of moral purpose in their organizations and beyond.

The message of this chapter is: Make your moral purpose more prominent and hitch it to the other four forces in this book, including making the complexity of change work in your favor. It is easy to lose one's way, even if motivated by moral purpose. The latter must be fueled by the power of a change culture. Immerse yourself in the change process and you will be less likely to go astray. I did say at the end of Chapter 1 that the culture of change beckons; now it's time for "beckon to become being." This is more than Gandhi's "Be the change you want to see in the world." Leading in a culture of change involves creating with others the change that you never knew you wanted.

Chapter Three

Nuance: Understanding Change

UNDERSTANDING THE CHANGE PROCESS IS LESS about innovation and more about innovativeness. It is less about strategy and more about strategizing. And it *is* rocket science, not least because we are inundated with complex, unclear, and often contradictory advice. Mickleth-wait and Wooldridge (1996) refer to management gurus as "witch doctors" (although they also acknowledge their value). Argyris (2000) talks about flawed advice. Mintzberg, Ahlstrand, and Lampel (1998) take us on a *Strategy Safari*. Drucker is reported to have said that people refer to *gurus* because they don't know how to spell *charlatan!*

Frame the Work as a Learning Problem, Not an Execution Problem

Effective change *is* a learning proposition (Google, 2019). This chapter is about insights into the nature of change.

Across the chapters and in the final chapter I will have more to say about leadership for change. For now I want to convey the mysteries and magic of change itself—ideas that we and others have learned over the years including more recently identifying change's nuances (Fullan, 2019).

Would you know what to do if you read Kotter's *Leading Change,* in which he proposes an eight-step process for initiating top-down transformation (1996, p. 21)?

1. Establish a sense of urgency.
2. Create a guiding coalition.
3. Develop a vision and strategy.
4. Communicate the change vision.
5. Empower broad-based action.
6. Generate short-term wins.
7. Consolidate gains and producing more change.
8. Anchor new approaches in the culture.

Would you still know what to do if you then turned to Beer, Eisenstat, and Spector's observations (1990) about drawing out bottom-up ideas and energies?

1. Mobilize commitment to change through joint diagnosis [with people in the organization] of business problems.
2. Develop a shared vision of how to organize and manage for competitiveness.
3. Foster concerns for the new vision, competence to enact it, and cohesion to move it along.

4. Spread revitalization to all departments without pushing it from the top.

5. Institutionalize revitalization through formal policies, systems, and structure.

6. Monitor and adjust strategies in response to problems in the revitalization process [cited in Mintzberg et al., 1998, p. 338].

What do you think of Hamel's advice (2000) to "lead the revolution" by being your own seer?

Step 1: Build a point of view.

Step 2: Write a manifesto.

Step 3: Create a coalition.

Step 4: Pick your targets and pick your moments.

Step 5: Co-opt and neutralize.

Step 6: Find a translator.

Step 7: Win small, win early, win often.

Step 8: Isolate, infiltrate, integrate.

And, after all this advice, if you did know what to do, would you be right? Probably not. The biggest problem is that there are no hints about *the process of change* that would accomplish the recommended goals. There is no notion of partnership (other than you should have some), or even taking into account the people who have to lead change on the ground. Some of the advice seems contradictory. (Should we emphasize top-down or bottom-up strategies?) Much of it is general and unclear about what to do—what Argyris (2000) calls "nonactionable advice." This is why many of us have concluded that change cannot be managed in a literal sense. It can be understood and perhaps led, but it cannot be controlled.

After taking us through a safari of 10 management schools of thought, Mintzberg et al. (1998) drew the same conclusion when they reflected that "the best way to 'manage' change is to allow for it to happen" (p. 324), "to be pulled by the concerns out there rather than being pushed by the concepts in here" (p. 373). It is not that management and leadership books don't contain valuable ideas—they do—but rather, that there is no "answer" to be found in them. Nevertheless, change can be led, and leadership does make a difference.

Becoming change savvy gets us into the socio-psychology of change, essentially forming your actions based on what you know or can come to know about the people that are part of the change process in which you are engaged. Recall that I have concluded that 80% of our best ideas come from leading practitioners. Mintzberg (2004) gets at this same point when it says that managing change "is as much about doing in order to think as thinking in order to do" (p. 10). In Mintzberg's terms effective leaders (managers he calls them) have to know that:

> through complex phenomena, they have to dig out information, they have to probe deeply in the ground, not from the top; (p. 52)
>
> Strategy is an interactive process, not a two-step sequence; it requires continual feedback between thought and action. Put differently, successful strategies are not immaculately conceived, they evolve from experience ... Strategists have to be in touch; they have to know what they are strategizing

about; they have to respond and react and adjust, often allowing strategies to *emerge*, step by step. In a word, they have to *learn*. (Mintzberg, 2004, italics in original)

Understanding change means understanding people—not people in general but people in specific (i.e., the ones you are leading right now). More Mintzberg:

Leadership is about energizing other people to make good decisions and do better things. In other words, it is about helping to release the positive energy that exists naturally within people. Effective leadership inspires more that empowers; it connects more than it controls; it demonstrates more than it decides. It does all of this by *engaging*—itself above all, and consequently others. (p. 143)

It seems elementary to say that change is about interaction with people, but that is exactly the essence of the matter. Have good ideas but process them, and get other ideas from those you work with, including—no, *especially*—those you want to change. We now know that the more complex the change, the more that people with the problem must be part of the solution.

Based on the past 40 years of studying and doing change my team and I have developed certain insights about the process of change. We have tested them against the research literature, and with others working closely in hundreds of change situations. I call the set of insights "the skinny on becoming change savvy" (Fullan, 2010; see Figure 3.1). Consider this list the wisdom of the crowd. Think of the nine strategies in concert, not as standalone.

1. Be right at the end of the meeting.
2. Relationships first (too fast, too slow).
3. Acknowledge the implementation dip.
4. Accelerate as you go.
5. Beware of fat plans.
6. Behaviors before beliefs.
7. Communication during implementation is paramount.
8. Excitement prior to implementation is fragile.
9. Become a lead learner.

Figure 3.1. Becoming change savvy.

1. Be Right at the End of the Meeting

As David Cote retired at the end of a long-distinguished career as CEO of Honeywell, he was asked, "What is the most important lesson you have learned about leadership?" This is what he said:

> Your job as a leader is to be right at the end of the meeting, not at the beginning of the meeting. It's your job to flush out all the facts, all the opinions ... because you'll get measured on whether you made a good decision, not whether it was your idea in the beginning.
>
> I have a reputation of being decisive. Most people would say that being decisive is what you want in a business leader, but it is possible for decisiveness to be a bad thing. With bigger decisions you make bigger mistakes. (Quoted in Bryant, 2013)

In a later publication I elevated this insight into the first principle of *nuance* (Fullan, 2019). Complex change must be approached as a matter of *joint determination*. The more complex the problem, the more that people with the problem must be part of solving the problem. This is not just a matter of commitment. It is that people with the problem will have some of the best insights—insights that can only be accessed through interaction between and among leaders and others in the situation.

2. Relationships First (Too Fast/Too Slow)

Think about the last time you were appointed to a new leadership position and you were heading for your first day on the job. These days, all newly appointed leaders, by definition, have a mandate to bring about change. The first problem the newcomer faces is the too-fast-too-slow dilemma. If the leader comes on too strong, the culture will rebel (and guess who is leaving town—cultures don't leave town). If the leader is overly respectful of the existing culture, he or she will become absorbed into the status quo. What to do? Take in the following good advice from Herold and Fedor (2008). Change-savvy leadership, they say, involves:

- Careful entry into the new setting;
- Listening to and learning from those who have been there longer;
- Engaging in fact-finding and joint problem solving;
- Carefully (rather than rashly) diagnosing the situation;
- Forthrightly addressing people's concerns;
- Being enthusiastic, genuine, and sincere about the change circumstances;
- Obtaining buy-in for what needs fixing; and
- Developing a credible plan for making that fix.

What should strike you is not the charismatic brilliance of the new leaders but their "careful entry," "listening," and "engaging in fact-finding and joint problem solving." In other words, attend to the new relationships that have to be developed. There are situations, of course, where the culture is so toxic that the leader may need to clean house. Or there might be one "derailer" that stands out, whom few like, and who requires immediate action (get the wrong people off the bus), but by and large, leaders must develop relationships first to a degree with the people in the situation before they can push challenges. You get only one chance to make a first impression, and it had better be a good one—not too fast, nor too slow.

Steve Munby, when he was appointed the CEO of the National College of School Leaders in England in 2001, knew about the too-fast-too-slow skinny. The National College had lost its focus under the previous CEO, trying to be all things to all people. Steve knew that refocusing was essential. He had some ideas, but the first thing he did was make 500 phone calls to school heads across the country asking them what the college meant to them, what it could do to serve them better, and so on. One month later (it takes a while to phone 500 people and make a personal connection), he had conveyed to the college that change was coming and that he was going to listen and act. The college went on to reestablish a strong presence in the field, helping to develop school leaders across the country and to prepare and support the next generation of school heads. He moved fast, but not too fast, and he was careful to build relationships as he went (Fullan, 2010, pp. 18–19).

Munby (2019) went on to write his professional autobiography that shows how he blended relationship building and organization development in three very different settings. Munby also shows that each new situation represents having to learn new things. His whole career, and it has been impressive, is captured in the title of his book, *Imperfect Leadership*. Each new context requires new learning. Humility and confidence seem to go hand in hand.

In my book *Nuance,* the finding is that effective leaders must become deeply "contextually literate"—they must understand with some depth the cultures in which they work. Now think of moving to a new position. My colleague Brendan Spillane from Western Australia provided this additional insight as we talked through nuance. He offered that every time a leader moves to a new organization or department, he or she becomes "automatically de-skilled," i.e., does not understand the new culture. Reconciling too fast/too slow is to understand the context as it is and as it could be. Not to be too literal, but we have found that it takes six months or so of immersion to gain some understanding of the context as you consider with others the nature of the change direction.

3. Acknowledge the Implementation Dip

At first, this seems obvious; then we can get more complicated. Herold and Fedor again have the insight, finding in business what we have found in education.

When you introduce something new, even if there is some preimplementation preparation, the first few months are bumpy. How could it be otherwise? New skills and understanding require a learning curve.

Figure 3.2 furnishes additional insights. First is the myth of change: that there will be some immediate gains. It can't

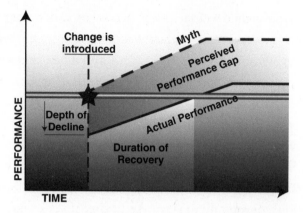

Figure 3.2. The myth and reality of change (Herold & Fedor, 2008).

be thus, by definition. Second, look inside the "depth of decline" triangle. If you are an implementer, the costs to you are immediate and concrete, while the benefits are distant and theoretical. In other words, the costs–benefits ratio is out of whack in favor of the negative. Third, if you are a leader, don't expect many compliments. People are not having a good time. Thus, leaders should be aware that their job is to help the organization get through the process to the point where benefits start to accrue. One way of thinking of change leadership is that the goal is to shorten the duration of the implementation dip to the point where benefits outweigh costs.

Let's return more pointedly to the human element. People are not widgets, even though many a leader wishes they were. Change stands or falls initially not on the cognitive rationale and understanding of the change but more on the emotional connection to the change. Change is "sticky" when it connects to people's emotions not their rational minds. The old adage that captures this is, "People may not remember what

you said, but they will remember how you made them feel."
To make matters more complicated, it is not that the "rational
proposers" are correct and the "emotional" responders are
wrong. We know that the former can be dead wrong and the
latter alive right. The dynamics of ideas and emotions via the
relationships of leaders and implementers contain the answer
to effective change.

In our work over the past two decades we have found that
the initial stages of change—say, those first few years—are
more complicated than we first had realized. Even if the
change is definable, the development of individual and collective capacity takes longer and requires greater effort than we
thought. For example, consider our work in California with
leaders across all levels. The state, the counties ($N = 58$),
and the districts ($N = 1009$) have broadly endorsed the
new direction since 2013. We are finding that "capacity to
implement" is still the major stumbling block—even though
the majority of implementers endorse the change (Fullan,
Rincón-Gallardo, & Gallagher, 2019).

Most often in these cases, there is agreement about the
change itself, followed by superficial implementation—and in
some cases, they are unaware that what they are doing is
superficial, believing that they are following the precepts of
the innovation. And, in turn, they may mistakenly reject the
innovation (we tried that …).

Another aspect of the dip is that many of the innovations
being pursued—say, those of deep learning (see Chapter 4)—
are indeed innovations where the initial phases entail working
out the nature of the change itself. It is more development
than dip.

4. Accelerate as You Go

Does the dip slow you down? If you ignore the dip and plow ahead, you have the illusion of change. On the other hand, if you dwell on the possibility of the dip, you may get nowhere. Sooner than later, the best way of building momentum is through purposeful action. Later in the chapter we will meet Wendy Thompson, who spent a whole year having local meetings with constituents, literally night after night getting ideas for a vision and strategic plan, and testing possibilities, only to find at the end of the year that only 20% of the people had heard there was a vision-building exercise, and most of them were against it.

Wendy Thompson had spent her time talking about hypothetical matters that had no meaning to the people in the constituency. It was all talk, without any action-based learning.

So getting to action sooner rather than later is key; it's not like you start things and wait for the implementation dip to play itself out. There is a great deal of activity that involves the leader. I used the label "go slow to go fast" to capture what needs to happen. Here is one of many examples we could use.

Michelle Pinchot, a principal in Garden Grove Unified School District, California led a successful turnaround effort in a school called K3 Peters, which had 600 children ages 5 to 9. When she arrived in 2011, school performance in literacy, for example, was stagnant. At the same time, the staff was congenial as a group but there was little in-depth focus. The school became successful within four years, reaching double-digit gains (11%) in a single year. We filmed the school as an example of success (see video, K3 Peters, www.michael fullan.ca). But this is not my main point.

In the summer of 2016, Michelle was transferred to another large elementary school in Garden Grove called Heritage that was low performing. We decided to conduct an experiment. I said to Michelle, "You know a lot about getting success; let's see how quickly that you and the staff can improve Heritage" (see also Fullan & Pinchot, 2018). I said that all I would do would be to ask her by email every six months for two years questions like: What was the lay of the land when you arrived in the summer of 2016? What did you decide to do for the first six months? Six months later, I send a similar note, and six months later asked, "How is it going? What's next?" And so on.

By the second year, the school increased literacy and math scores, as measured by the new state test. The district conducts an annual climate survey that is based on criteria of an effective learning environment. Table 3.1 displays the results.

The changes in culture are stunning given that they occurred within two years. How did Pinchot and her staff do it? At a general level, they focused on many of the specific

Table 3.1. Heritage Staff Responses, 2016–2018

	2016	2017	2018
Students feel safe at school.	71%	94%	94%
Site leadership fosters professional growth and feedback.	30%	86%	100%
This school promotes trust and collegiality among staff.	68%	88%	100%
This school has a safe environment for giving peer-to-peer feedback.	44%	93%	100%
Students ask questions when they don't understand.	33%	71%	86%

strategies of focused collaboration that we examine in the next chapter.

Michelle exemplified many of the attributes that we see in lead learners. She spent the first several months setting the stage (we need to do something about literacy, and we will do it together); she established permanent teams led by teachers (in which she participated); she enabled collaborative teams to observe, collect information, and help solve problems.

Michelle Pinchot embodies several of what we have come to call our "sticky phrases" about change (insights that are powerful and stick with you). Here are three:

1. "Go slow to go fast" (what seemed slow in the first six months was tantamount to "start your engines").

2. "Use the group to change the group" (multiple groups were focused; Michelle was present and enabling; new teachers leadership in particular groups flourished).

3. "Talk the walk" (more and more teachers (and students) learn to explain what they are doing and why). If people talk the walk every day to each other, it is a sign that both specific things are happening and that people are learning every day (our change in culture; interaction and talk the walk is daily, not just episodic).

In short, *leading in a culture of change* leaders don't think of the implementation dip per se. They believe that they are in the early stages of a rapidly improving enterprise that is highly challenging but exciting because it is working with others to do something that is crucial, and that brings people to new heights of accomplishment and pride. When it works, leaders are just as happy for the adults as they are for the students and their families.

5. Beware of Fat Plans

We have found that there is a tendency for leaders to over plan on paper. Our colleague Doug Reeves (2009, p. 81) captures this phenomenon wonderfully: "The size and prettiness of the plan is inversely related to the quality of action and the impact on student learning." Later Reeves (2019) wrote a book on "finding your leadership focus," where he showed that too many ideas lead to the "law of initiative fatigue." "Too fat or too many" ideas at the front end overloads the change process.

From 2000 to 2009, we worked with York Region (a very large multicultural district just north of Toronto). The district started with a 45-page implementation plan in 2007, then a 22-page plan in 2008, and an 8-page plan in 2009. In the course of this decade, York Region became one of the top-five performing school districts in the province of Ontario. It seems that the more you know, the briefer you get when it comes to plans. The emphasis shifts to action early and throughout the process. As we will see in Chapter 6, shared coherence is what matters, and you get this from specific action guided by brief focused documents, not from large documents.

Why are planning and plans so seductive? There are no *people* on the pages! PowerPoint slides don't talk back. We meet John Malloy a few times in this book; he is the director (superintendent) of the mammoth Toronto District School

Board (TDSB) with its 583 schools. When he first arrived he observed, "I inherited a culture that expected templates, recipes, and road maps." TDSB had the greatest documents and planning guides in the world of education; but they came and went. Malloy replaced the system of elaborate written plans with a system of interaction build around focused goals and briefer documents. You can test the efficacy of your written plans by asking implementers to "talk the walk" with each other with the goal of making the plans "living documents" (see the Malloy case study in Fullan, 2019, pp. 51–61).

6. Behavior before Beliefs

Don't be too literal. Of course, beliefs matter and leaders should work on them from day one. But if the issue is changing beliefs, you want to use the stimulant of new behavior early in the process. This phenomenon goes back at least to Leonardo da Vinci, whom I have called "the patron saint of nuance" (Fullan, 2019). Leonardo referred to himself as a *discepolo della sperientia* or a disciple of experience and experiment. "My intention is to consult experience first," he wrote in his notes (Isaacson, 2017). Da Vinci wanted detail so that his ideas could expand from that basis.

Recall earlier when I discussed how one might change a teacher's beliefs about whether all children (his or her students, for example) could learn. I showed that such beliefs would not be shaken by research evidence, or moral exhortation, but rather, through having new experiences in relatively nonthreatening circumstances with help from a leader or peer whereby his or her students responded differently (i.e., they started learning).

It's a far cry from da Vinci to Jamie Oliver, but the comparison fits. Jamie was stymied with the problem of changing eating habits of secondary school students from obviously unhealthy choices (as in, you get sick or reduce your life span). His first challenge was Nora, the head dinner lady, who would have no part of his fancy ways. She has over 1,000 mouths to feed, on time, and at 37 pence a stomach. He tried to work alongside Nora but couldn't do anything right according to her. Partly for his own sanity ("I have to get out of her kitchen"), and partly to have her experience what it was like to cook properly, he arranged her to spend a week working with his chefs at his famous London restaurant called Fifteen. The chief chef, Arthur Potts, began to teach Nora basic knife skills in cutting vegetables; then he moved on to not overcooking, and then to a rule she had never heard of: never send a dish out that you have not tasted. She did taste one of Arthur's dishes, but it was so delicious that she sat down and ate the whole bowl. Gradually, these new behaviors began to make sense to Nora. She altered her beliefs, and working with Jamie altered the eating habits of an entire secondary school.

We see another of our sticky phrases in action here: "Go outside to get better inside." Many people have not had experience outside of their own setting. The culture they are in reinforces their blinkered vision. Give people new experience in relatively nonthreatening circumstances and give them an opportunity to talk about it with others and peers.

Change is strange sometimes because it is not always logical. How many times have you heard the litany of reactions to an obviously promising idea: It won't work here; we tried that; we don't have time; and so on. I slightly (but only slightly) exaggerate in saying: If you want to kill a good idea, mandate it! You are far better off to expose people to good ideas, use the group to change the group, and participate as a learner. The change moral is, "Give people experience in the new way," as a starting point for considering particular changes.

7. Communication During Implementation Is Paramount

Another way of thinking about guidelines 1–6 is to worry early about what might happen during implementation, don't talk about change too long before moving ahead, and once you do, start a change increase communication from day one.

Consider Wendy Thompson, whom I referred to above. Several years ago, Thompson was appointed the chief executive of Newham Council, a very large municipality in England. She spent a whole year conducting forums of discussion about a new vision, talking to thousands of people, only to find from a survey after 12 months that 80% of the people had never heard of the vision, and of the remaining 20%, 80% of them were against the vision. A year's hard work produces 4% in favor!

Our newest finding about leadership corroborates this lesson (communication during implementation is paramount). Leaders who "participate as learners" with staff in moving the organization forward have the most impact (Fullan, 2014, 2017). Once change starts in practice, the leader better be there!

Communication during implementation serves a double function. On the one hand, it gives the leader an opportunity to learn how implementation is going. As the leader gets specific insights about what is working, he or she can feed that back in both small and large forums. On the other hand, problems get identified more readily and can be addressed.

When you come to think about it, almost everything I say in *Motion Leadership* is about "leading in a culture of change." It is about ongoing daily, focused, inside-and-out communication *while doing the work*.

8. Excitement Prior to Implementation Is Fragile

Maybe this is what is meant by the phrase "anticipation is greater than fulfillment." How often have you witnessed or been part of a group where members declare: "I'm in! Let's do it," and variations on the theme. The point is not to dampen initial enthusiasm, but rather to realize that genuine excitement comes from accomplishing something, not imagining it. Thus, knowledgeable leaders strive for small early successes, acknowledge real problems, admit mistakes, protect their people, and celebrate success along the way. The other eight insights in this chapter all channel change into accomplishments worth celebrating. Even setbacks are seen as problems to be solved, resulting in an even greater sense of fulfillment once they are addressed. Guideline 8 is a reality check, so that quality implementation is treated as problematic.

Successful change is a crescendo, not a rally. In successful cases, people work gradually at first, and then with greater intensity as they reach a culminating point of success where it is obvious, for example, that students are learning and producing at levels never before achieved. Organizations work toward and celebrate their periodic crescendos, and avoid faking them through empty celebrations.

9. Become a Lead Learner

Lead learner is the theme across the chapters of this book, so I need only identify the parameters here. It consists of six overlapping aspects:

1. Participating as a learner.
2. Listen, learn, and lead, in that order.
3. Be an expert and an apprentice.
4. Develop others to the point that you become dispensable.
5. Be relentlessly persistent and courageous about impact.
6. Focus on the "how" as well as the "what" of change.

Leading change is about helping others focus and learn. As we move into an era where more innovation is required, not the least because existing institutions are failing, we need leaders who will help the group achieve new, more effective steady states with the parallel capacity of adjusting to and taking advantage of new opportunities. Recall Schein's definition of culture: "constantly processing with the group external factors and internal integration" in relation to core goals (moral purpose).

Once you have your house in dynamic order, it is easier to maintain the stance toward continuous improvement and innovation. The important point is to be in charge of your own development, and in many ways to please external constituents simultaneously. There is an increasing number of challenges in the environment, but there are also more opportunities. Leading in a culture of change represents new external and internal dynamics.

Our own "deep learning" is a case in point (Fullan, Quinn, & McEachen, 2018). We start with the finding that the status quo—the way schools are—is no longer fit for purpose. Almost four out of five students are disengaged from school learning, inequity is rapidly on the rise, anxiety and stress among the young of all socioeconomic groups is steadily increasing. All signs point to change. But what change? We have worked with some schools around the world to develop a model of change that consists of six global competencies (character, citizenship, collaboration, communication, creativity, and critical thinking) and four aspects of the learning environment.

While many school leaders have joined us, it is clear that it takes a certain amount of risk taking (getting out of one's comfort zone) to develop the new ideas under conditions of uncertainty and doubt on the part of others. More and more, we can predict that leaders will have to operate under conditions of growing problems on the one hand and uncertain solutions on the other. Leaders will need all five leadership stances as they proceed through the next decade and more.

Conclusion

As leaders contemplate alternatives, it is probably good for them to rethink resistance. We are more likely to learn something from people who disagree with us than we are from people who agree. But we tend to hang around with and over-listen to people who agree with us, and we prefer to avoid and under-listen to those who don't. Not a bad strategy for getting through the day, but a lousy one for getting through the implementation dynamics.

Resisters are crucial when it comes to the politics of implementation. In democratic organizations, such as universities, being alert to differences of opinion is absolutely vital. Many a strong dean who otherwise did not respect resistance has been unceremoniously run out of town. In all organizations, respecting resistance is essential, because if you ignore it, it is only a matter of time before it takes its toll, perhaps during implementation, if not earlier.

For all these reasons, successful organizations don't go with only like-minded innovators; they deliberately build in differences. They don't mind so much when others—not just themselves—disturb the equilibrium. They also trust the learning process they set up—the focus on moral purpose, the attention to the change process, the building of relationships, the sharing and critical scrutiny of deep knowledge, and traversing the edge of chaos while seeking coherence.

The nine ideas for becoming change savvy are intended to first loosen up your thinking about the phenomenon of change, and then as a set to help you focus more realistically— more humanly—on the phenomenon of change. Now that we have an appreciation of the process of change, we can turn to more details. One of the most powerful and complex variables involves the role of teams and groups. We have some great new insights, for example, about autonomy and collaboration. Almost everyone agrees that "relationships" are key, but they seem to leave it as a truism. It is time we delved into its deeper and more specific meaning when it comes to the dynamics of change.

Chapter Four

Relationships, Relationships, Relationships

I F MORAL PURPOSE IS JOB ONE, RELATIONSHIPS ARE job two, as you can't get anywhere without them. If you asked someone in a successful enterprise what caused the success, the answer almost always is, "It's the people." But that's only partially true: It is actually the *relationships* that make the difference.

In pursuing the importance of relationships in this chapter, I will do something different. Let's talk about businesses as if they had souls and hearts, and about schools as if they had minds. We will see that moral purpose, relationships, and organizational success are closely interrelated. We will also find that businesses and schools have much in common. Businesses are well advised to boost their moral purpose—for their own good as well as for the good of society. Schools, particularly because we live in the knowledge society, need to strengthen their intellectual and social (group) quality as they deepen their moral purpose. We will conclude with what businesses and schools, in fact what all successful organizations, have in common, namely, "learning is the work" is their center of gravity.

Businesses as If They Had Souls

In "Relationships: The New Bottom Line in Business," the first chapter of their book *The Soul at Work*, Lewin and Regine (2000) talk about complexity science:

> This new science, we found in our work, leads to a new theory of business that places people and relationships—how people interact with each other, the kinds of relationships they form—into dramatic relief. In a linear world, things may exist independently of each other, and when they interact, they do so in simple, predictable ways. In a nonlinear, dynamic world, everything exists only in relationship to everything else, and the interactions among agents in the system lead to complex, unpredictable outcomes. In this world, interactions, or relationships, among its agents is the organizing principle. (pp. 18–19)

For Lewin and Regine, relationships are not just a product of networking but "genuine relationships based on authenticity and care." The "soul at work" is both individual and collective:

> Actually, most people want to be part of their organization; they want to know the organization's purpose; they want to make a difference. When the individual soul is connected

to the organization, people become connected to something deeper—the desire to contribute to a larger purpose, to feel they are part of a greater whole, a web of connection. (p. 27)

It is time, say Lewin and Regine, to alter our perspective: "to pay as much attention to how we treat people—co-workers, subordinates, customers—as we now typically pay attention to structures, strategies, and statistics" (p. 27). Lewin and Regine make the case that there is a new style of leadership in successful companies—one that focuses on people and relationships as essential to getting sustained results.

It's a new style in that it says, place more emphasis than you have previously on the micro level of things in your company, because this is a creative conduit for influencing many aspects of the macro level concerns, such as strategy and the economic bottom line. It's a new style in that it encourages the emergence of a culture that is more open and caring. It's a new style in that it does not readily lend itself to being turned into "fix it" packages that are the stuff of much management consultancy, because it requires genuine connection with co-workers; you can't fake it and expect to get results. (p. 57)

Many other studies along the way have shown that companies that place high value on the quality of their employees end up doing best in the market. Recall that Sisodia, Wolfe, and Sheth (2007) identified *firms of endearment*, drawing their sample by developing a list of companies that met their "humanistic performance criterion," that is, these companies paid equal attention to all five stakeholders (customers, employees, investors, partners, and society). Sisodia and his colleagues then examined the financial performance of these companies using the Standard and Poor's performance index over a 10-year period. They found that the firms of endearment outperformed the S&P index by 122% over that period. Several other studies have produced similar results.

These results do not just show that some companies produce better results because they are nice to employees. Most of all, they create and support the conditions for employees to be successful. As I said in *The Six Secrets of Change,* the best way for employers "to love their employees" is to create the conditions for their success. We have already seen in Chapter 1 that businesses have a very poor track in establishing the conditions for success. Chamorro-Premusic provides a nice twist on assessing leaders when he argues that "to judge leaders talent, we need to objectively consider their teams' performance" (p. 123). Put positively, he says, "The key goal of a leader should be to help the team outperform its rivals" (p. 122).

Other business authors echo the newly founded emphasis on relationships: Bishop (2000) argues that leadership in the twenty-first century must move from a product-first formula to a relationship-first formula; Goffee and Jones (2000) ask, "Why should anyone be led by you?" Their answer is that we should be led by those who inspire us by

- Selectively showing their weaknesses (revealing humanity and vulnerability);
- Relying on intuition (interpreting emergent data);

- Managing with tough empathy (caring intensely about employees and about the work they do); and

- Revealing their differences (showing what is unique about themselves).

This sets us up to consider schools. This question is more than a matter of "minds." It also relates to the question of the quality of relationships in schools.

Schools as If They Had Minds

The key question is, do schools have *collective* minds? It turns out that this is a tricky question, and its answer seems encouraging, at least in the argument. The course of the argument goes in two parts: (i) a promising start; and (ii) autonomy, collaboration, and the promise of more.

A Promising Start: 1990s

Nothing presents a clearer example of school district reculturing than School District 2 in New York City. Elmore and Burney (1999, pp. 264–265) provide the context:

District 2 is one of thirty-two community school districts in New York City that have primary responsibility for elementary and middle schools. District 2 has twenty-four elementary schools, seven junior high or intermediate schools, and seventeen so-called Option Schools, which are alternative schools organized around themes with a variety of different grade configurations. District 2 has one of the most diverse student populations of any community district in the city.

It includes some of the highest-priced residential and com-
mercial real estate in the world, on the Upper East Side of
Manhattan, and some of the most densely populated poorer
communities in the city, in Chinatown in Lower Manhattan
and in Hell's Kitchen on the West Side. The student population of the district is twenty-two thousand, of whom about
29 percent are white, 14 percent black, about 22 percent
Hispanic, 34 percent Asian, and less than 1 percent Native
American.

Anthony Alvarado became superintendent of District 2 in
1987. At that time, the district ranked tenth in reading and
fourth in mathematics out of 32 subdistricts. Eight years later,
by 1996, it ranked second in both reading and mathematics.
Elmore and Burney describe Alvarado's approach:

> Over the eight years of Alvarado's tenure in District 2, the
> district has evolved a strategy for the use of professional
> development to improve teaching and learning in schools.
> This strategy consists of a set of organizing principles about
> the process of systemic change and the role of professional
> development in that process, and a set of specific activities,
> or models of staff development, that focus on systemwide
> improvement of instruction (1999, p. 266).

The seven organizing principles of the reform strategy are
as follows:

1. It's about instruction and only instruction.
2. Instructional improvement is a long, multistage
   process involving awareness, planning,
   implementation, and reflection.

3. Shared expertise is the driver of instructional change.

4. The focus is on systemwide improvement.

5. Good ideas come from talented people working together.

6. Set clear expectations, then decentralize.

7. Collegiality, caring, and respect are paramount.

Elmore and Burney (1999, p. 272) explain:

In District 2, professional development is a management strategy rather than a specialized administrative function. Professional development is what administrative leaders do when they are doing their jobs, not a specialized function that some people in the organization do and others do not. Instructional improvement is the main purpose of district administration, and professional development is the chief means of achieving that purpose. Anyone with line administrative responsibility in the organization has responsibility for professional development as a central part of his or her job description. Anyone with staff responsibility has the responsibility to support those who are engaged in staff development. It is impossible to disentangle professional development from general management in District 2 because the two are synonymous for all practical purposes.

So, it looked like District 2 was an out-and-out success. And it was in its own right, but it did not last nor did the concepts travel well. Alvardo went on in 1998 to become Chancellor of Instruction (reporting to a Superintendent) at

San Diego Unified School district and left in 2003 under a cloud of dissatisfaction and little success.

My point here is that this is part of a bigger story. We know that quality relationships and focused teamwork result in success. Schools are caring institutions that should have a leg up on this, but care by itself does not lead to increased performance. It has also been the case that studies of collaboration and "professional learning communities" as they are often called have been going on for four decades. So far they have proven little. I suspect the reason is that the quality of collaboration has been superficial and uneven.

Learning Is the Work

Let's shift focus and gears. What if we thought of the main function of organizations as "learning is the work"? When learning is confined to workshops, training, performance appraisals, and the like, we see the intended learning as one or more steps removed from actually doing the work.

Every important point in this book brings us back to culture. Culture is the way we do things around here. In successful organizations, the culture is based on daily learning built into daily interaction. Think of it this way: it is what happens in between meetings or workshops that counts.

Frederick Taylor is known as the father of scientific management. According to Taylor's studies in the steel industry, work tasks could be broken down, and workers could be taught to perform them with maximum efficiency and productivity. Taylor (2007) developed four principles of scientific management:

1. Replace rule-of-thumb work methods with methods based on scientific study of tasks.

2. Scientifically select, train, and develop each worker rather than passively leaving them to train themselves.

3. Cooperate with workers to ensure that the scientific methods are followed.

4. Divide work nearly equally between managers and workers so that the managers apply scientific management principles to planning the work and workers actually performing the tasks (p. 31).

Taylor was on the right track, but his approach was too literal and dehumanized to say the least. He was right about precision, but wrong about prescription. Taylor sought *prescription*; today, we want to figure out how to get consistent *precision* without imposing it. And we want it all—precision and innovation. Now that Tiger Woods is back in good graces, we can recall his Accenture ad: "Relentless consistency, 50%; willingness to change, 50%."

The essence of learning is the work that concerns how organizations address their core goals and tasks with relentless consistency, while at the same time learning continuously how to get better and better at what they are doing through innovation and refinement.

Atul Gwande is a general surgeon at the Brigham and Women's Hospital in Boston. Let's start with a seemingly straightforward innovation: doctors and nurses regularly washing their hands. In his book *Better*, Gwande (2007) reports that every year, 2 million Americans acquire an infection while they are in a hospital, and 90,000 die from that infection. Yet one of the greatest difficulties that hospitals have "is getting clinicians like me to do the one thing that consistently halts the spread of infections: wash your hands" (p. 14). Hospital statistics show that "we doctors and nurses wash our hands one-third to one-half as often as we are supposed to" (p. 15).

As we will see with each of the examples in this chapter, successful workers mobilize themselves to be "all over the practices that are known to make a difference." In Gwande's seemingly simple problem, it took consistent education, conveniences of hand-washing facilities, and frequent random spot checks to monitor and improve performance on something as simple as washing one's hands regularly.

We see time and again that new technology (in this case, hand-washing dispensers) is not sufficient to spur behavioral breakthroughs. Technology is at best an accelerator; culture is the driver.

Toyota has made a science of improving performance. The essence of Toyota's approach to improved performance in all areas of work consists of three components:

1. Identify critical knowledge.
2. Transfer knowledge using job instruction.
3. Verify learning and success. (Liker & Meier, 2007)

This is not a "project, but rather a process that will require continued, sustained effort *forever*" (Liker & Meier, 2007, p. 82, italics in original). Welcome to "learning is the work"!

Liker and Meier make the critical point that going about identifying and standardizing critical knowledge is not just for technical tasks, such as those performed on assembly lines. To illustrate, they use three examples: manufacturing (bumper molder operator), a nurse in a busy hospital, and an entry-level design engineer. This universal applicability is a key message: consistency and innovation can and must go together, and you can achieve them though organized learning in context.

Liker and Meier estimate "that Toyota spends five times as much detailing work methods and developing talent in employees as any other as any other company we have seen" (p. 110). Then: "If we were to identify the single greatest difference between Toyota and other organizations (this includes service, healthcare and manufacturing organizations), it would be the *depth of understanding* among Toyota employees regarding their work" (p. 112, italics added).

On the question of whether focusing on the consistency of practice inhibits creativity, Liker and Meier reflect: Is Toyota producing "mindless conformity or intentional mindfulness?" Their response: Toyota places a very high value on "creativity, thinking ability and problem-solving" (p. 113). When the preoccupation is with the science of improving performance, you can be like Tiger Woods: nail down the common practices that work in relation to getting consistent results; *at the same time*, you are freeing up energy for working on innovative practices that get even greater results, including taking timeouts for major overhaul of what you are doing, as Tiger has done four times in his career.

The intent of standardized work is not to make all work highly repetitive, giving license to neo-Taylorites to robotize every tasks. Rather, the goal is to define the best methods for reducing "bad variation" (ineffective practice) in favor of practices that prove to be effective. We are not talking about 100% of the work. In most cases, write Liker and Meier, "the critical aspects of any work equal about 15–20% of the total work" (p. 143). The key is to identity those tasks and to take special care that everyone does those tasks well using the known best method of doing so. And "for these items there is no acceptable deviation from the defined method" (p. 144).

Liker and Meier (2007) then apply the approach to the tasks of a busy hospital nurse. After categorizing all aspects of the job into "core" and "ancillary" tasks, they break them down into routine and nonroutine elements. For example: starting an IV in a peripheral vein consists of six steps:

1. Stabilize the vein.
2. Place the tip of the needle against the skin.
3. Depress the skin with the needle.
4. Puncture skin with needle.
5. Change needle angle.
6. Advance the catheter.

For each of the six steps the authors identify "key points" with respect to safety, quality, technique, and cost.

No part of the work of consistent effective performance is static. In the midst of any action there is constant learning, whether it consists of detecting and correcting common errors or discovering new ways to improve. Let's make a return visit to education.

Education as a Slow Learner

I don't want to dis the work on collaboration between 1990 and the present—indeed, I have been part of much of it. Quite frankly, the yield from the work on collaboration in education has been limited. This is not to say that no good work has been done, only to indicate that on the ground it has not established the empirical case that effective collaboration is on the rise in school systems. My point in this section is twofold: There are both normative and practical obstacles to collaboration in schools; and recently there are signs as to what specific forms of collaboration are most likely to be effective.

All we have so far in education is that collaboration is probably a good thing. Actually, it isn't necessarily so. People can collaborate to do nothing or to do the wrong thing. The good news is that the research in the last three or four years has begun to pinpoint the ways in which collaboration can be effective. Not quite like Toyota, but with a good focus on precision. It starts with sorting out the relationship between autonomy and collaboration. Teachers have long argued for the importance of teacher autonomy. Others have called for more teamwork. It turns out to be a false dichotomy. Autonomy is not isolation. The latter is usually bad for you—whether at work or in life-long periods of isolation, resulting in decline. What if we thought of it differently? Today I am autonomous and have my ideas. Tomorrow I am with the group and contribute to it as well as learn from it, and so on. The idea is that you don't choose between autonomy and collaboration. You do both.

The most recent research—one could say research reported over the past three or four years—has given us much more specificity and clarity about the role of collaboration. I use five such studies here: the works of John Hattie and the related research of Jenni Donohoo and Steven Katz, Andy Hargreaves and colleagues, Amanda Datnow, Susan Moore Johnson (SMJ), and the Maori scholar from New Zealand, Russell Bishop.

John Hattie became famous 15 years ago in education by producing his meta-study analysis of "visible learning"— what teaching practices produced the best learning on the part of students. Feedback to students, teaching students to think about how they learn (meta-learning), and prior achievement were a few of the factors that had statistically significant effects (in the 0.4 to 0.5 effect size range). As Hattie pointed out, these effect sizes were modest but worth taking into account. A few of us pointed out that all the practices were "individualistic" endeavors. We asked, "What was the impact of collaborative activities?"

Hattie turned his attention to collective work and found indeed that it was much more powerful in its impact on student learning—a whopping 1.57 coefficient, much larger than he had ever found (Donohoo, Hattie, & Eells, 2018). The big question then became, "What is "collective efficacy?" Hattie and associated researchers found that it consisted of four factors: shared belief among teachers that they would produce results; primary reason was "evidence of impact"; a culture of collaboration to implement high-yield teaching strategies; and a leader who participates in frequent, specific collaboration. These four factors are consistent with our findings. Focus on powerful levers, enable all to engage, use peers to strengthen practice, and appoint leaders who participate in strengthening what works.

Donohoo & Katz (2020) proceeded to conduct a more thorough study of collective efficacy. The latter consists of the grounded belief that a group (of teachers for example) can make a difference in learning for all students—a belief that is based on cause and effect knowledge, goal-directed actions, and progressive inquiry (linking action, instructional improvement, and learning results). Increased collective efficacy as such is causally linked to measurable higher student achievement. Donohoo and Katz show what collective efficacy is, how it can be learned, and what impact it has on higher student achievement.

During this same period, Andy Hargreaves and his co-worker Michael O'Connor (2018) studied professional learning networks in seven countries. To start with, they said there is a big difference between "collaborative professionalism" and "professional collaboration." The latter referred to professionals getting together (to do whatever); the former concerned collaboration that was based on "professionalism." Specifically, they found that collaborative professionalism involved these issues:

- The joint work of teachers is embedded in the culture and life of the school.
- Educators care for each other as fellow professionals as they pursue their challenging work.
- They collaborate in ways that are responsive to and inclusive of the culture of their student, themselves, the community, and society (Chapter 9).

Similarly, Datnow and Park compared two high-poverty schools in California with two that were not successful. The difference, they said, was in the exact purpose and nature of collaboration. In the two successful schools there was specific "pedagogical" and "emotional" support. With respect to the former:

- Teachers didn't distinguish between formal and informal collaboration.
- There are candid, deliberative, supportive norms.

- They strive for continuous innovation and improvement.

- There is collective sense-making and integration of curriculum policy and existing practice (Chapter 3).

Datnow and Park (2019) also found a strong theme related to emotional support:

- Be buffered from external demands.

- Be a source for inspiration for improving practice.

- Lighten the burden around curriculum design and planning.

- Be a site for celebrating student learning (Chapter 6).

Another long-standing scholar of school cultures is Susan Moore Johnson (SMJ) from Harvard, who has also garnered new insights by going deeper into successful school cultures. One of the background studies that SMJ and her colleagues conducted was to trace 50 new teachers over a four-year period. They found that one-third had left teaching altogether and another third had changed schools. Teachers in low-income schools were less likely to benefit from mentoring and support than teachers from high-income schools, and thus less likely to continue as teachers.

As we will see later about hiring employees and appointing new leaders, most organizations pay scant careful attention to what they are doing and getting (see Cappelli: "Your approach to hiring is all wrong," 2019). By contrast, in successful schools SMJ found major differences. These schools saw new hiring as a crucial part of the success of the schools. She lists the best practices in these schools (Johnson, 2019):

- Make fit a priority.
- Mission fit was essential.
- Endorsing the school's practices counted.
- Professional norms and practices matter.
- Expectations for ongoing development and collaboration were explicit.
- Invest in the recruitment and hiring process.
- Recruit a diverse pool of candidates from various sources.
- Screen candidates carefully.
- Organize school visits and interviews.
- Require a teaching demonstration and a debrief meeting (pp. 37–45).

As SMJ concludes: "This group of successful schools was remarkable in that each had developed a multi-step recruitment and hiring approach that engaged educators throughout the school in meeting and assessing candidates" (p. 46).

When it comes to collaboration, all schools studied by SMJ and her colleagues had teams of teachers working together, but there was a world of difference between the successful and nonsuccessful schools. In the latter schools, teachers "criticized their teams, saying that they didn't help them teach better, were misaligned with their school's larger purpose and programs, or focused excessively on improving test scores" (p. 86). Once again, collaboration per se is not the point.

By contrast, in the successful schools (note that all of the schools studied by SMJ were high-poverty, low-performing schools), principals and teacher teams worked together in setting aspirational purpose, promoting shared learning, not lockstep execution, and providing a psychologically safe environment for teams (pp. 89–90).

There is more: Teachers relied on their teams; cohort teams addressed students' needs, behavior, and organizational culture; aspirational purpose was well honed, sufficient predictable time was available to work together; ongoing, engaged support from administrators occurred; and there was ongoing facilitation by trained school leaders.

All of the schools in SMJ's study were located in the same state (Massachusetts). All three of the successful schools "improved rapidly" and "achieved the state's highest rating" (p. 97).

In sum, compared to earlier work (say, 2000–2015), the new collaborative work is built into the daily culture, is more specific, addresses both pedagogical and emotional support, and is linked directly to student learning. It is still limited in at least two ways: successful cases are very much in the minority, and we are just seeing "school change," not change in districts or larger systems. Quality collaboration, in other words, is small scale and limited.

What we are witnessing in SMJs and other studies of effective collaboration are the exception and in an indirect way the failure of what I would call the narrow "human capital" strategy that I characterized as a "wrong driver" (Fullan, 2011). SMJ makes the same point in referring to the

Rand evaluation of the Bill & Melinda Gates Foundation $575 million intervention in three large urban districts and four clusters of charter schools (Stecher et al., 2018). Despite the massive funds and ongoing evaluation and monitoring of the effort, "it failed to achieve its goals, having no appreciable benefits for students' achievement on standardized tests or their graduation rates" (Johnson, 2019, p. 234).

SMJ concludes:

> Although it was ambitious, the strategy itself was too narrowly conceived, focusing on individual teachers while ignoring the schools in which they worked … This strategy does nothing to improve how those teachers do their work together in the context of the school—for example, ensuring that goals for student's learning are understood and shared by everyone, recognizing how their interactions with students both inside and outside class affect the school's culture, considering how well their curriculum and instruction align with what children experience within and between grades, establishing ways to track student progress through the school's program over time, and interacting with parents in ways that contribute to a better home–school relationship. (p. 234)

We see in the SMJ research that success requires a wholesale change in *culture*. Schools can mimic aspects of the required changes, as they engage in superficial collaboration that they inevitably find is not worth their time. I would estimate that fewer than 15% of schools and 10% of districts reflect the changes that SMJ is talking about. After 150 years of regular schooling, old cultures die hard!

One final reinforcer comes from Russell Bishop (2019), the Maori educator from New Zealand. He subtitles his book appropriately: "Relationship-Based Learning in Practice." Bishop spent over 12 years working with 50 New Zealand secondary schools building cultures of "establishing extended-family like relationships [that] are fundamental to improving Indigenous Maori students' educational achievement" (p. xiv). Bishop shows clearly that "relationships are fundamental to learning," especially for minority groups, and doubly especially for indigenous cultures that value personal relationships. But more than that, humans are hard-wired to learn through social connections. Bishop clearly shows that all students, and especially those least connected to regular schooling, require meaningful relationships in order to learn and develop.

Bishop (2019) found another aspect of traditional teaching culture that blocked change:

> While many teachers took on board the need to develop positive extended family-like relationships in their classrooms, they did not follow it up be taking on board the need to change their teaching practices from traditional to dialogic and interactive. (pp. 29–30)

Bishop found that despite overall success in a publicly funded multiyear initiative he failed to garner continued funding. Bishop acknowledges that he did not pay sufficient attention to certain critical "sustainability factors," including problems of developing sufficient and/or sustained capacity in teachers, problems with details of effective interactions, principal turnover, and the overall problem of lack of developing collective efficacy (pp. 37–47).

Bishop's overall model provides additional grist for the mill of deep and focused cultures of learning. He advocates three big action guidelines for leaders (Bishop 2019):

1. Leaders create and extended family-like context for learning.

2. Leaders interact within this context of learning.

3. Leaders monitor the progress of learners' learning and the impact of the processes of learning (Chapter 8).

I have labeled this section as "education as a slow learner" in order to stress the point that we have known quite a lot about collaboration for some 50 years. Only lately—in the past five years or so—are we beginning to decipher the details and specificity with respect to the change in culture that will be required. This still represents to me an uphill battle, but at least we are in the game.

In the meantime, I would like to reinforce the critical point about "learning is the work" with another way of expressing it, namely, "learning in context."

Learning in Context

To be blunt: learn in context or learn superficially. When it comes to context it seems that the focus on human capital—the quality of the individual—blinds us to the critical role of context. As Elmore (2000, pp. 2–5) notes:

> Attempting to recruit and reward good people is helpful to organizational performance, but it is not the main point. Providing a good deal of training is useful, but that too is a limited strategy.

Elmore (2000) tells us why focusing only on talented individuals will not work:

> What's missing in this view [focusing on talented individuals] is any recognition that improvement is more of a function of *learning to do the right thing in the setting where you work* than it is of what you know when you start to do the work. Improvement at scale is largely a property of organizations, not of the pre-existing traits of the individuals who work in them. Organizations that improve do so because they create and nurture agreement on what is worth achieving, and they set in motion the internal processes by which people progressively learn how to do what they need to do in order to achieve what is worthwhile. Importantly, such organizations select, reward and retain people based on their willingness to engage the purposes of the organization and to acquire the learning that is required to achieve those purposes. Improvement occurs through organized social learning... Experimentation and discovery can be harnessed to social learning by connecting people with new ideas to each other in an environment in which ideas are subject to scrutiny, measured against the collective purposes of the organization, and tested by the history of what has already been learned and is known. (p. 25; emphasis added)

This is a fantastic insight: learning in the setting where you work, or learning in context, is the learning with the greatest payoff because it is more specific (customized to the situation) and because it is social (involves the group).

Learning in context is developing leadership and improving the organization as you go. Such learning changes the individual and the context simultaneously.

Human capital is ineffective unless it is coupled with its "more difficult to do" partner of changing the culture. Human capital at best is a short-term strategy. In education, to the extent that ongoing learning is addressed it is usually through professional development, workshops, and other external events. Sometimes learning is via PLCs (professional learning communities) or COLS (community of learners), which may appear to be part of context but are often episodic—a bit like saying, "I do something meaningful with my partner on Tuesdays." Our Australian colleague Peter Cole (2004) ruefully calls professional development "a great way to avoid change" because it appears that learning is taking place, but little else happens *in between workshops*. Professional development programs or courses, even when they are good in themselves, are removed from the setting in which teachers work. At best, they represent a useful input, but only that. Once more, it is what happens day after day that counts—in the setting in which one works.

The remaining point to make is that the key factors identified in this chapter operate as a constellation of forces, (i.e., they feed on each other) as mutual strengths generate even more spinoffs because of the interaction effects. This is what Jim Collins was getting at in his identification of the "flywheel," which he revisited in a recent brief monograph (Collins, 2019). The flywheel consists of a constellation of five or so key interrelated factors (e.g., hiring good people, having a focused collaborative culture, etc.). At the beginning, says Collins:

> It feels like turning a giant, heavy flywheel. Pushing with great effort you get the flywheel to inch forward ... You don't stop you keep pushing. The flywheel moves a bit faster ... [it] builds momentum ... then at some point—breakthrough! The flywheel flies forward with unstoppable momentum. (Collins, 2019, p. 1)

In other words, the heavy lifting of establishing a new focused collaborative culture is at the beginning—that critical first year. In year two, some momentum occurs, then in year three the payoff becomes evident and you get what Collins calls "the power of strategic compounding" (p. 1).

Collins stresses that it is not a list of static objectives, but rather, how one factor ignites another to accelerate momentum. Collins describes the case of Deb Gustafson, an elementary school principal in Kansas. Before examining the content of Gustafson's flywheel, Collins makes a key point that we will take up in Chapter 6 on "coherence"—something we call "leadership from the middle," where the middle (schools, school districts, regional jurisdictions) does not wait for the top to initiate change: "Gustafson didn't wait for the district superintendent or the Kansas Commissioner of Education ... to fix the entire system. She threw herself into creating a unit-level flywheel right there in her individual school" (p. 13). The particular flywheel Gustafson ended up with consisted of six factors (Figure 4.1).

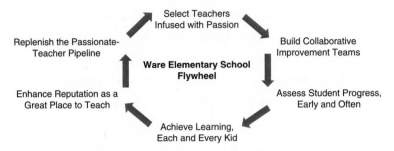

Figure 4.1. Ware elementary school flywheel.

At this point, Gustafson has 15 years under her belt. She stresses, "It's about culture, and the relationships and the collaboration with your teammates to improve and deliver for the kids—all that made us attractive to the right people" (p. 14).

In essence, the message of this chapter is that culture is core; that culture consists of a constellation of definable factors related to "learning is the work," such as those on Figure 4.1. The work is hardest in the beginning, but propels forward faster by feeding the flywheel with inputs that have accelerating impact on what is already a powerful force.

One more example: Laura Schwalm was appointed superintendent of Garden Grove Unified School District (GGUSD) in Anaheim, California, in 1999. When she started, GGUSD was one of the lowest-performing districts in the state with a highly diverse and high-poverty student population of over 40,000 students. When Laura retired in 2013, GGUSD was one of the highest-performing districts in the state. How did she and her colleagues do it? In effect, Laura and her team built a better farm. One of her favorite sayings is, "Not only can you lead a horse to water, you can 'salt the oats' and they will drink."

Laura and I now work together, and one of our current themes in relation school district improvement is, "What does getting serious about getting serious look like?" (compared to superficial reform). In Chapter 6 on coherence making, I will show you what we have so far. It's all about context.

Conclusion

With respect to leadership, there is still a strong case to be made for recruiting good individuals to the organization, and I will take up this matter in Chapter 7 when we examine the leadership continuum.

In the meantime, several key conclusions are warranted. There is more to relationships than relationships. Effective relationships have a certain quality. They have a strong emotional component (supporting each other when times are tough or individuals are down). And they have a *getting better at the daily work* dimension (striving for good consistency about what works and seeking innovations that make performance all the more effective). There is a constellation of a small number of factors related to changing culture that can serve as a flywheel in Collin's sense, thereby accelerating quality change once these factors are established.

I mentioned above—building better farms. There is an old song from World War I with the lyrics "How ya going to keep them down on the farm once they've seen Paree?" Learning in context raises the alternative, "How ya going to keep them down on the farm once they've seen the farm?" If the farm is no good, they are not going to stay long (read teacher turnover). Good farms provide good contexts for learning. People want to stay in contexts of learning—because they grow, because they get more done, because they are emotionally committed to others and to the mission of the place. Get this right and you have won more than half the battle.

Relationships are central to success but must develop toward greater mutual commitment and specificity related to the purpose of the work. From a change perspective, there is an interesting side benefit. In good collaborative work, you don't have to impose ideas because they are built into the culture. Quality collaborative cultures produce precision of practice without having to resort to prescription. Only changes in daily culture are strong enough to alter behavior and beliefs.

When cultures fundamentally improve in the way I have been describing in this chapter, the added bonus is that *organizational accountability* becomes established. I have called traditional approaches to accountability (tests linked to rewards and punishment) a "wrong" policy driver (because it backfires). Our focus on transparent and specific use of performance data turns accountability on its head as use of evidence becomes part of everyday work. Elmore (2004) put it this way:

> Investments in internal accountability must logically precede any expectation that schools will respond productively to external pressure for performance. (p. 15)

In our "leading in a culture of change" we have built in accountability within the day-to-day interactions. In *Nuance* I called this a "culture-based accountability." It includes the use of external data, and when required, external intervention—the latter is used selectively (i.e., when persistent failure occurs or in cases of fiscal and other malfeasance). Internal accountability works because it is transparent, specific, nonjudgmental, and above all, because people can see what is going on as they build mutual commitment to getting results. The latter—making progress—propels them to do even more.

Where the world is heading (where it needs to head) makes businesses and schools less different than they have been in the past. These days both businesses and schools need to be concerned with moral purpose and good ideas if they are to be successful and sustainable organizations. The laws of nature and the new laws of sustainable human organizations (corporations and public schools alike) are on the same evolutionary path. To be successful beyond the very short run, all organizations must incorporate moral purpose; respect, build, and draw on human relationships; and foster purposeful collaboration inside and outside the organization. Doing these things is for the good of the organization, and for the good of us all. Getting collaboration right is central to cultures of change.

Chapter Five

Knowledge Building and Deep Learning

THE COVER STORY IN THE BUSINESS SECTION OF THE Toronto Globe and Mail was titled "Knowledge Officer Aims to Spread the Word" (2000a). In its profile of Rod McKay, international chief knowledge officer at KPMG, the article said, "McKay's challenge is to get KPMG's 107,000 employees at all levels worldwide to share information" (p. M1). "Knowledge sharing," says McKay, "is a core value within KPMG. Every individual is assessed on their willingness to share their experience with others in the firm" (p. M1).

Knowledge building, knowledge sharing, knowledge creation, knowledge management. Is this just another fad? New buzzwords for the twenty-first century? They could easily become so unless we understand the role of knowledge in organizational performance and set up the corresponding mechanisms and practices that make knowledge sharing a cultural value.

Information is machines. Knowledge is people. Information becomes knowledge only when it takes on a "social life" (Brown & Duguid, 2000). By emphasizing the sheer quantity of information, the technocrats have it exactly wrong: if only we can provide greater access to more and more information for more and more individuals, we have it made. Not so! Instead what you get is information glut.

Brown and Duguid (2000) establish the foundation for viewing knowledge as a social phenomenon:

> Knowledge lies less in its databases than in its people. (p. 121)
>
> For all information's independence and extent, it is people, in their communities, organizations and institutions, who ultimately decide what it all means and why it matters. (p. 18)
>
> A viable system must embrace not just the technological system, but the social system—the people, organizations, and institutions involved. (p. 60)
>
> Knowledge is something we digest rather than merely hold. It entails the knower's understanding and some degree of commitment (p. 120)

If you remember one thing about information, it is that it only becomes valuable in a *social context*.

> Attending too closely to information overlooks the social context that helps people understand what that information might mean and why it matters. (p. 5)

[E]nvisioned change will not happen or will not be fruitful until people look beyond the simplicities of information and individuals to the complexities of learning, knowledge, judgement, communities, organizations, and institutions. (p. 213)

Incidentally, focusing on information rather than use is why sending individuals and even teams to external training by itself does not work. Leading in a culture of change does not mean placing changed individuals into unchanged environments. Rather, change leaders work on changing the context, helping create new settings conducive to learning and sharing that learning.

Most organizations have invested heavily in technology and possibly training, but hardly at all in knowledge sharing and creation. And when they do attempt to share and use new knowledge, they find it enormously difficult. Take the seemingly obvious notion of sharing best practices within an organization. Identifying the practices usually goes reasonably well, but when it comes to transferring and using the knowledge, the organization often flounders. Hewlett-Packard attempted "to raise quality levels around the globe by identifying and circulating the best practices within the firm" (Brown & Duguid, 2000, p. 123). The effort became so frustrating that it prompted Lew Platt, chairman of HP, to wryly observe, "if only we knew what we know at HP" (cited in Brown & Duguid, p. 123).

In this chapter, we will see several examples of knowledge-creation and sharing from business and education. These organizations and schools are still in the minority, but they are the wave of the future. (And what we can learn from them dovetails perfectly with the discussion in previous chapters.) I will also describe major advances in deep learning that we are making in our multi-country initiative "new pedagogies in deep learning for deep learning" (Fullan, Quinn, & McEachen, 2018).

Examples from Business

In their study of successful Japanese companies, Nonaka and Takeuchi (1995) explain that these companies were successful not because of their use of technology but rather because of their skills and expertise at *organizational knowledge creation,* which the authors define as "the capability of a company as a whole to create new knowledge, disseminate it throughout the organization, and embody it in products, services and systems" (p. 3).

> Building on earlier work by Polyani (1983), Nonaka and Takeuchi make the crucial distinction between *explicit knowledge* (words and numbers that can be communicated in the form of data and information) and *tacit knowledge* (skills, beliefs, and understanding that are below the level of awareness): "[Japanese companies] recognize that the knowledge expressed in words and numbers represents only the tip of the iceberg. They view knowledge as being primarily 'tacit'—something not easily visible and expressible. Tacit knowledge is highly personal and hard to formalize, making it difficult to communicate or share with others. Subjective insights, intuitions, and hunches fall into this category of knowledge. Furthermore, tacit knowledge is deeply rooted in an individual's action and experience, as well as in the ideals, values, or emotions that

he or she embraces" (p. 8). Successful organizations access tacit knowledge. Their success is found in the intricate interaction inside and outside the organization—interaction that converts tacit knowledge to explicit knowledge on an ongoing basis. My book *Nuance* makes exactly this point. Effective leaders—and I provide 10 case study examples in *Nuance*—get below the surface, helping others to do so. They constantly get at knowledge in context where (as we saw in the previous chapter) learning becomes the work.

The process of knowledge creation is no easy task. First, tacit knowledge is by definition hard to get at. Second, the process must sort out and yield quality ideas; not all tacit knowledge is useful. Third, quality ideas must be retained, shared, and used throughout the organization.

As Nonaka and Takeuchi (1995) say,

> The sharing of tacit knowledge among multiple individuals with different backgrounds, perspectives, and motivations becomes the critical step for organizational knowledge creation to take place. The individuals' emotions, feelings, and mental models have to be shared to build mutual trust. (p. 85)

In further, more comprehensive work, von Krogh, Ichijo, and Nonaka (2000) subtitle their book "how to unlock the mystery of tacit knowledge and release the power of innovation." Lamenting the overuse of information technology per se, von Krogh et al. take us on a journey that is none other than an explanation of how effective companies combine care or moral purpose with an understanding of the change process and an emphasis on developing relationships (corresponding, of course, to Chapters 2 through 4 in this book)—again, ideas we delved into in Chapter 4.

> Knowledge enabling includes facilitating relationships and conversations as well as sharing local knowledge across an organization or beyond geographic and cultural borders. At a deeper level, however, it relies on a new sense of emotional knowledge and care in the organization, one that highlights how people treat each other and encourages creativity. (von Krogh et al., 2000, p. 4)

Knowledge, as distinct from information, "is closely attached to human emotions, aspirations, hopes, and intention" (von Krogh et al., 2000, p. 30). In other words, there is an explicit and intimate link between knowledge building and internal commitment on the way to making good things happen (see Figure 1.1 in Chapter 1).

I will soon take up the not-so-straightforward chicken-and-egg question of the causal relationship between collaborative work cultures and knowledge sharing, but let's stay for a moment with the conditions under which people share knowledge. Von Krogh et al. elaborate:

> Knowledge creation puts particular demands on organizational relationships. In order to share personal knowledge, individuals must rely on others to listen and react to their ideas. Constructive and helpful relations enable people to share their insights and freely discuss their concerns. They also enable micro communities, the origin of knowledge creation in companies, to form and self-organize. Good relationships purge a knowledge-creation process of distrust,

fear, and dissatisfaction, and allow organizational members to feel safe enough to explore the unknown territories of new markets, new customers, new products, and new manufacturing technologies. (p. 45)

Von Krogh et al. (2000) emphasize that a culture of care is vital for successful performance, which they define in five dimensions: mutual trust, active empathy, access to help, lenience in judgment, and courage. We have already seen some of these terms in Chapter 4 where we found that cultures in highly effective schools provide both technical and emotional support to system members. Similarly, the US Army, KPMG, Gemini Consulting, Monsanto, British Petroleum, Sears, and a host of other companies in "tough" businesses espouse quality relationships as vital to their success.

Many of us have experienced firsthand the consequences of not attending to these matters. Von Krogh et al. (2000, pp. 56–57) summarize Darrah's study (1993) of a computer components supplier. The company faced severe productivity and quality problems. Management's response was to punish ignorance and lack of expertise among factory-floor workers; at the same time, whenever they ran into manufacturing problems, it explicitly discouraged them from seeking help from the engineers who designed the components and organized the production line. These workers gained individual knowledge as best they could. They worked on sequentially defined manufacturing tasks and tried to come to terms with the task at hand, without thinking through the consequences for the performance of other tasks at other stages of the manufacturing process. When a new worker was employed, he received little training. Yet for productivity and cost reasons, the novice would be put to work as soon as possible. Knowledge transactions between workers and engineers were very rare, and most of the knowledge on the factory floor remained tacit and individual. The tacit quality of individual knowledge was pushed even farther because the foremen would not allow personal notes or drawings to help solve tasks.

Concerned with the severe productivity and quality problems, a new production director suggested a training program for factory workers that would help remedy the situation. The program was designed in a traditional teaching manner: The product and manufacturing engineers were supposed to explain the product design and give an overall view of the manufacturing process and requirements for each step. At the end of the training session, the engineers would ask the workers for their opinions and constructive input—a knowledge transaction intended to improve quality and communication. The workers, however, knew the consequences of expressing ignorance and incompetence, and they did not discuss the problems they experienced, even if they knew those problems resulted from flaws in product design. Nor did they have a legitimate language in which to express their concerns and argue "on the same level" as the engineers. The workers mostly remained silent, the training program did not have the desired effects, and the director left the company shortly thereafter.

What about the causal relationship between good relationships and knowledge sharing? Most people automatically assume that you build relationships first and information will flow. Von Krogh et al. (2000) seem to accept this causal direction: "We believe a broad acceptance of the emotional lives of others is crucial for establishing good working relationships—and good relations, in turn, lead to effective knowledge creation" (p. 51). However, I would venture to say, and again refer to Chapter 4, effective cognitive and emotional support occurs simultaneously. There is no separation of sequence between the two. They feed on each other in a virtuous spiral.

Von Krogh et al. (2000) draw the same conclusion when they talk about two interrelated responsibilities: "From our standpoint, a 'caring expert' is an organizational member who reaches her level of personal mastery in tacit and explicit knowledge *and* understands that she is responsible for sharing the process" (p. 52, emphasis in original).

Figure 5.1 illustrates the elements of knowledge exchange. Knowledge is constantly received and given, as organizations provide opportunity to do so and value and reward individuals as they engage in the receiving and sharing of knowledge. The logic of what we are talking about should be clear: (i) complex, turbulent environments constantly generate messiness and reams of ideas; (ii) interacting individuals are the key to accessing and sorting out these ideas; (iii) individuals will not engage in sharing unless they find it motivating to do so (whether because they feel valued and

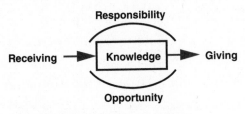

Figure 5.1. Knowledge-sharing paradigm.

are valued, because they are getting something in return, or because they want to contribute to a bigger vision).

Leaders in a culture of change realize that accessing tacit knowledge is crucial and that such access cannot be mandated. Effective leaders understand the value and role of knowledge creation; they make it a priority and set about establishing and reinforcing habits of knowledge exchange among organizational members. To do this, they must create many mechanisms for people to engage in this new behavior and to learn to value it. Control freaks need not apply: people need elbow room to uncover and sort out best ideas. Leaders must learn to trust the processes they set up, looking for promising patterns and looking to continually refine and identify procedures for maximizing valuable sharing. Knowledge activation, as von Krogh et al. (2000) call it, "is about enabling, not controlling ... anyone who wants to be a knowledge activist must give up, at the outset, the idea of controlling knowledge creation" (p. 158). They elaborate:

> From an enabling perspective, knowledge that is transferred from other parts of the company should be thought of as a source of inspiration and insights for a local business operation, not a direct order that must be followed. Control of knowledge is local, tied to local recreation ... The local unit uses the received knowledge as input to spark its own continuing knowledge-creation process. (p. 213)

It is important to note that companies must *name* knowledge sharing as a core value and then establish mechanisms and procedures that embody the value in action. Dixon (2000) provides several illustrations. One involves British Petroleum:

> British Petroleum's Peer Assist Program. Peer Assist enables a team that is working on a project to call upon another team (or a group of individuals) that has had experience in the same type of task. The teams meet face-to-face for one to three days in order to work through an issue the first team is facing. For example, a team that is drilling in deep water off the coast of Norway can ask for an "assist" from a team that has had experience in deep-water drilling in the gulf of Mexico. As the label implies, "assists" are held between peers, not with supervisors or corporate "helpers." The idea of Peer Assists was put forward by a corporate task force in late 1994, and BP wisely chose to offer it as a simple idea without specifying rules or lengthy "how-to" steps. It is left up to the team asking for the assistance to specify who it would like to work with, what it wants help on, and at what stage in the project it could use the help. (p. 9)

That was 1994. In 2010, we see the danger of relying on ad hoc success stories when BP was responsible for one of the largest environmental disasters in history as it failed to control an explosion and consequent series of oil leaks in the Gulf of Mexico—the biggest leak in history, discharging some 4.9 million barrels (210 million US gallons) into a massive area, taking several years to control. BP was eventually convicted of gross negligence and reckless conduct and fined $42 billion, not to mention additional lawsuits. Peer-to-peer assistance is a good idea for using lateral knowledge, but it must be governed by an overall system of moral purpose and oversight.

Probably the best-known example of leveraging knowledge within a team is the US Army's use of after-action review (AARs). The AARs are held at the end of any team or unit action with the intent of reusing what has been learned immediately in the next battle or project. These brief meetings are attended by everyone who was engaged in the effort, regardless of rank. The US Army's simple guidelines for conducting AARs are (i) no sugar coating, (ii) discover ground truth, (iii) no thin skins, (iv) take notes, and (v) call it like you see it. The meetings are facilitated by someone in the unit, sometimes the ranking officer, but just as often another member of the team. The learning from these meetings is captured both by the members, who all write and keep personal notes about what they need to do differently, and by the facilitator, who captures on a flip chart or chalkboard what the unit as a whole determines that it needs to do differently in the next engagement. Army AARs have standardized three key questions: What was supposed to happen? What happened? And what accounts for the difference? An AAR may last 15 minutes or an hour, depending on the action that is being discussed, but in any case, it is not a lengthy meeting.

Bechtel's Steam Generator Replacement Group also uses this practice, although it calls the meetings "lessons learned" instead of AARs. Bechtel is a multibillion-dollar international engineering, procurement, and construction company engaged in large-scale projects, such as power plants, petrochemical facilities, airports, mining facilities, and major infrastructure projects. Unlike other parts of Bechtel in which individuals work in ever-changing project teams, the Steam Generator Replacement Group is a small specialized unit that works on a lot of jobs together. Anything learned on one job can be immediately used by the team on the next job. The nature of its work leaves little room for error. The average window of time to replace a steam generator is 70 days or less, unlike the typical Bechtel project, which may last two years or more. This unforgiving schedule mandates that the Steam Generator Replacement Group learn from its own lessons, because even a small mistake can result in a significant delay to a project. The lessons are captured in two ways: first, in weekly meetings to which supervisors are required to bring lessons learned; then, at the end of each project, the project manager brings all players together for a full day to focus on the lessons learned (pp. 37–40).

The design criteria underlying these examples are crucial:

1. They focus on the intended user(s).

2. They are parsimonious (no lengthy written statements or meetings).

3. They try to get at tacit knowledge (this is why personal interaction or exchange is key and why dissemination of "products" or explicit knowledge by itself is rarely sufficient).

4. Learning takes place "in context" with other members of the organization.

5. They do not aim for faithful replication or control.

With the advances in technology and artificial intelligence (AI), clearly the role of knowledge has become much more complex and problematic to harness. Two of the leading experts on new technologies are McAfee & Brynjolfsson. In *Harnessing the Digital World* (2017), they analyze the explosive and interactive development of *Machines, Platforms and Crowds*. Machines consist of the expansive capabilities of digital creations; platforms involve the organization and distribution of information; and crowds refer to "the startling amount of human knowledge, expertise, and enthusiasm distributed all over the world and now available, and able to be focused online" (p. 14). McAfee and Brynjolfsson suggest that successful enterprises will be those that integrate and leverage the new triadic set (machines, platforms, and crowds) to do things very differently than what we do today. If we don't learn this new way of learning and working, we "will meet the same fate of those that stuck with steam power" (p. 24).

In a similar vein, the start-up specialist Eric Ries says that adaptability is all the more necessary because the environment is awash with radical changes and unpredictability. Ries then comments on his experiences as an entrepreneur in developing and consulting with startups:

> I have come to realize in today's organizations—both established and emerging—are missing capabilities that are needed for every organization to thrive on the century ahead: the ability to experiment rapidly with new products and new business models, the ability to empower their most creative people, and the ability to engage again and again in an innovation process—and manage it with rigor and accountability—so that they can unlock new sources of growth and productivity. (p. 3)

The long and the short of the situation, according to McAfee and Brynjolfsson, is there is no reliable playbook for what to do because "there is simply too much change and too much uncertainty at present" (p. 27). They argue that the best way forward is to "predict less, experiment more." We are back to the culture of change: Build the capacity to change through "external adaptation and internal integration."

Knowledge and Education

As some people observe, you can get any fact you want from Google. It has become increasingly clear that knowledge utilization is not that simple. Given, students can become whizzes at technology and access to information but still not be very smart when it comes to making insightful observations, let alone taking solid decisions and actions about life.

Acquiring sheer knowledge doesn't seem to be the answer. For one thing, students are incredibly bored at the prospect. I referred earlier to the fact that students are less and less engaged as they go up the grades, as the following graph shows. Lee Jenkins asked several thousand teachers at different grade levels "what percentage of your students are enthused about learning." He found a steady decline from kindergarten to grade 9 where barely more than a third of students found learning worthwhile (Figure 5.2).

In 2014, we decided to act on the knowledge that the present system wasn't working spurred on by the interest of some schools and district or system leaders that wanted to change the public education. We formed a global partnership we called "new pedagogies for deep learning." We had a framework for action that guided the work and intended the

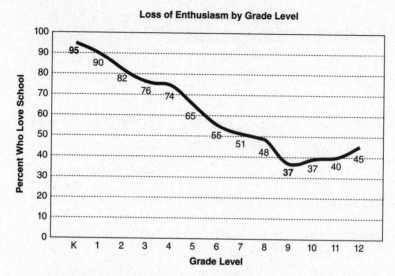

Figure 5.2. Loss of enthusiasm (Lee Jenkins, 2012).

"product" would come from the partnership. We started with the 6Cs, called the "global competencies":

- *Character*—Proactive stance toward life and learning to learn, grit, tenacity, perseverance and resilience, empathy, compassion, and integrity in action.

- *Citizenship*—A global perspective, commitment to human equity and well-being through empathy and compassion for diverse values and worldviews, genuine interest in human and environmental sustainability, solving ambiguous and complex problems in the real world to benefit citizens.

- *Collaboration*—Working interdependently as a team; interpersonal and team-related skills; social, emotional, and intercultural skills; managing team dynamics and challenges.

- *Communication*—Communication designed for audience and impact, message advocates a purpose and makes an impact, reflection to further develop and improve communication, voice and identity expressed to advance humanity.

- *Creativity*—Economic and social entrepreneurialism, asking the right inquiry questions, pursuing and expressing novel ideas and solutions, leadership to turn ideas into action.

- *Critical thinking*—Evaluating information and arguments, making connections, and identifying patterns, meaningful knowledge construction, experimenting, reflecting, and taking action on ideas in the real world.

Over the past five years we have worked with over 1,200 schools in eight countries or regions (subsets of schools worked with us, some sponsored by the government, but most coming from clusters and the regional or local levels: Australia, Canada, Finland, Hong Kong Netherlands, New Zealand, Uruguay, and United States). The full model is simple and complex at the same time (Figure 5.3).

We have already seen the 6 Cs that are the center of Figure 5.3 labeled as deep learning. In turn, the Cs are guided by a four-part learning model (partnerships, pedagogical

Figure 5.3. Deep learning.

practices, learning environment, and leveraging digital), and supported by organizational and system conditions (school, region, state). All 13 of these components (6 Cs, 4 learning supports, and 3 system supports) have detailed rubrics enabling the use or application of the elements. Schools are supported on an ongoing basis by local cluster leaders with whom our central team works. The result has been thousands of learning examples from schools of the model in action (see also Quinn, McEachen, Fullan, Gardner, & Drummy, 2020).

Let's take two examples out of literally 1,000 or more I could select. The first, from Australia, is called "Young Minds of the Future," where three elementary schools worked together for three years "to develop ideas that would benefit the world." The second is a school-district-wide deep-learning endeavor in Avon Maitland District School Board (AMDSB) in Western Ontario that helped engage disconnected students in meaningful learning.

Young Minds of the Future Expo

Ringwood North Public School, Canterbury Public School, and Chatham Public School; Victoria, Australia

The Young Minds of the Future (YMF) exhibition was a student-led exhibition held on September 9, 2016, at Canterbury Primary School. This was the culmination of a truly collaborative learning experience for both students and teachers across three primary schools: Ringwood, Canterbury, and Chatham. This learning experience gave participants the opportunity to explore the concept of future and how the past has shaped our world and influences the years to come. Students brainstormed different areas of interest such as health, sport, education, gaming, food, and transport, and then compiled a list of questions they were curious about. Based on the list, teachers created a series of tutorials planned using iTunes U. Students signed up to attend the tutorials they were interested in. Students learned about augmented and virtual reality, child app developers, technological advances in sports, different modes of transport and their impact on the environment, sustainable fashion trends, and more. Working in teams, students chose an area to focus on and were required to predict what the future of their chosen field would look like based on findings from tutorials attended, as well as their individual research. Predictions were to be shared at the YMF exhibition. Students worked through a keynote to document and guide their learning and checked in regularly with their allocated teacher. Working together, students came up with what their YMF exhibition would focus on, why this idea was important, what research supported their claims, what their stall would look like, and how they would engage and interact with their audience on the day (p. 66).

Our video, Young Minds of the Future clearly shows the enthusiasm and crystal-clear articulation (what we call the capacity to "talk the walk") by students of what they are doing, why, and with what results (for the video see http://www.npdl.global).

In Ontario, Canada we pick up the story of Gabe (pseudonym).

Gabe: Avon Maitland District School Board

Gabe is a high school student who usually enrolled in nonacademic classes geared for the workplace stream. At the urging of one of his teachers, he recently enrolled in an academic Introductory Kinesiology course because he loves sports. He didn't think he would do well but stayed with it because he loved basketball and had a strong connection with the teacher who taught the course. Through her participation with the deep learning inquiry pedagogy, this teacher had redesigned many of the learning tasks to allow students more choice on what they learned and how they demonstrated their understanding of the curriculum expectations.

As an example of a deep learning task, the students were to explore the nutrition needs of an elite sports team of their choosing and create a nutrition supplement from all natural ingredients that would help athletes prepare for and/or recover from intense competition. During a class "marketing forum," students had to promote their nutrition products to industry experts who they had invited to get feedback. Community members such as a former professional hockey player, cross-fit gym owner, and a runner who recently completed the Boston Marathon sampled their products and asked questions about their learning. Gabe surprised himself with his commitment to this course. He said he was able to learn deeply about the topic because he was learning something that he was passionate about. He said he felt more engaged and confident and was able to demonstrate the depth of his learning. Gabe explained that he was proud of his work, and now felt that he could learn alongside peers—a feeling that he had not had before.

Gabe is part of our working hypothesis that "deep learning" is valuable for all students but is especially effective with students who have been previously disconnected from school and from learning. There are several key points to be made about our deep learning initiative. First, it dramatically caught the interest of students and teachers and those who worked with them. It caused new energy for learning, covered the basics of literacy and math, and created countless "applied" projects. Second (again, us learning from the field), we labeled the work "Engage the World, Change the World," essentially discovering that once they got going, most students wanted to work on some aspect of a local or global issue, learn about it in teams, and draw conclusions that reflect deep understanding and an aptitude for improvement.

We ended up defining deep learning as having these characteristics:

- Learning that sticks with you the rest of your life
- Learning that connects with passion
- Learning that is team related
- Learning that has significance for the world
- Learning that involves higher-order skills

We also identified what we ended up calling "emergent discoveries" that included the following themes:

- Helping humanity.
- Life and learning merge.
- Students are change agents.
- Working with others is an intense motivator.
- Character, citizenship, and creativity are catalytic Cs.
- Attack equity with deep learning.

We are learning some other things about how to lead in a culture of change (for more detail on the above, see Fullan et al., 2018). How, for example, do you change a stodgy system (boring schooling) into a new enterprise? Part of the answer is to identify a problem and provide the direction of a solution with accompanying supports. We also wondered how much support would be needed to be effective. We developed "tools" in the form of rubrics to guide the key elements of the model. It turned out that these were essential. Participants told us "the tools help us focus" without suffocating local initiative. We have just taken a step to move this forward with another publication, called *Dive into Deep Learning: Tools for Engagement* (Quinn et al., 2020).

Part and parcel of all this, as you will have surmised, is that the role of teachers and students relative to each other and to knowledge has radically changed closer to the worlds that McAfee, Brynjolfsson, and Ries portrayed ("predict less, experiment more").

For teachers, we see in Table 5.1 that the knowledge role is squarely as partners being "activators, culture builders, and collaborators."

These radical alterations in learning, especially in the role of knowledge relative to the roles of students and teachers, have been corroborated in a thorough study of deep learning by Jal Mehta and Sarah Fine (2019). First, despite following promising leads, Mehta and Fine found disappointingly few examples of deep learning in US high schools. This mainly confirms that the knowledge revolution has not infiltrated into the cultures of schools.

Digging deeper (no pun intended), Mehta and Fine did discover examples of deep learning. Some of these were at what

Table 5.1. A New Role for Teachers

Activator	Culture builder	Collaborator
Establish challenging learning goals, success criteria, and deep learning tasks that create and use knowledge.	Establish norms of trust and risk-taking that foster innovation and creativity.	Connect meaningfully with students, family, and community.
Access a repertoire of pedagogical practices to meet varying needs and contexts.	Build on student interests and needs. Engage student voice and agency as co-designers of the learning.	Engage with colleagues in designing and assessing the process of deep learning using collaborative inquiry.
Provide effective feedback to activate next level of learning.	Cultivate learning environments that support students to persevere, to exercise self-control, and to feel they belong.	Build and share knowledge of the new pedagogies and the ways they impact learning.

the authors call "the periphery"—in after-hours programs, theater clubs, and sports. A few instances were found in the odd classroom. In these cases, we see that the new role of knowledge is very different in terms of its nature and the roles of teacher and the student, respectively (Table 5.2).

Now we see a more dynamic role of students as creators and investigators of knowledge, passionately pursuing their interests with teachers as enablers and collaborators. Whether any of the above represents the beginning of a new cultural revolution in education remains to be seen. If it does,

Table 5.2.   Differences in Teaching Practice

Traditional teachers	Deep-learning teachers
Knowledge as certain	Knowledge as uncertain
Cover the material	Do the work of the field or domain
Student as receiver of knowledge	Student as creator of knowledge
Ethos of compliance	Ethos of rigor and joy

Note. Mehta and Fine (2019, p. 351).

its success will require all of the ideas in leading cultures of change that I have been amassing in this book.

Conclusion

Using education as the focus, the point of all this is that guided deep learning greatly increases the relevance of schooling; it galvanizes students into studying and action. It integrates moral purpose, relationships, and detailed learning. It provides a frame of learning that is good for all students but is especially good for those students who are disaffected from regular schooling (which turns out to be a higher percentage than Jenkins found, as more and more students find that the desperate race for grades is alienating). It finds common ground between education and business and education. It prepares students for the future that turns out to be now, not tomorrow.

In short, this foray into deep learning epitomizes a great deal of what is crucial about knowledge seeking, and what it is like to lead in a world where there is a glut of information, and a massive challenge to make sense of it for learning, and for the world at large. The changes are radical and relentless, and are of a different character than we have seen before. They are unpredictable. They are dangerous, played out in a troubled world. Knowledge is deeper, more dynamic, and in the service of transformation, not just improvement. Success will depend on more of us figuring out how to master the themes in this book.

I now turn to one of the most powerful needs in our framework: how to increase our capacity for *coherence making*—a theme that we have worked on diligently for the past decade.

Chapter Six
Coherence Making

CHANGE IS A LEADER'S FRIEND, BUT IT HAS A SPLIT
personality: its nonlinear messiness gets us into trouble.
But the experience of this messiness is necessary in order to
discover the hidden benefits—creative ideas and novel solutions are often generated when the status quo is disrupted. If
you are working on mastering the four leadership capacities
we have already discussed—moral purpose, understanding
change, developing team-based relationships, and building
deep knowledge—you need to figure out how to integrate
them. The mechanism for so doing is *coherence making*. This
concept has become so important since I first wrote about
it in 2001 that we have written a whole book on the topic
(Fullan & Quinn, 2016). But first, let's set it up.

Striving for Complexity and Achieving Clutter

Humankind is capable of great rational thought, which turns out to be a liability. In the candy shop of change we want it all! Doug Reeves (2009) calls the problem initativitiis; many things ad hoc, one by one seemingly desirable. In education we have called these "Christmas tree" schools—so many superficial adornments.

Morieux and Tollman (2014) tell us that it is the same in business. The subtitle of their book is "how to manage complexity without getting complicated." The authors were part of a group that created the "Complexity Index" by tracking the number of performance requirements at a representative sample of companies in the US and Europe from 1955 to 2010. The index shows that business complexity has multiplied sixfold over that period of 55 years. They state:

> The real curse is not complexity so much as 'complicatedness' by which we mean the proliferation of cumbersome organizational mechanisms—structures, procedures, rules and roles—that companies put in place to deal with the mounting complexity of modern business. (p. 5)

Delving further into the number of procedures and rules, Morieux and Tollman calculated that a 6.7% increase annually in new procedures over the 55-year period resulted in a 35-fold increase. They reckon that managers in the top quartile spend 30–60% of their time coordinating meetings and writing reports—"work upon work" they call it. Touching base on one of our other indicators—engagement—Morieux and Tollman found that employees in organizations that scored high on the complexity index were three times more likely to be disengaged in their work. Further, the percentage of Americans who are satisfied with their work declined from 61% in 1987 to 47% in 2011.

Broadly speaking they argue that the solution is to develop cultures based on "autonomy and cooperation" (which the reader will notice is precisely what I concluded in Chapter 4 of this book). As they put it:

> The simple rules do not aim at controlling employees by imposing formal guidelines and processes, rather, they create an environment in which employees work together to develop creative solutions to complex challenges. (p. 18)

All of this is compatible with what I have been saying throughout this book. In the book *Coherence: The Right Drivers in Action for Schools, Districts, and Systems,* Joanne Quinn and I addressed coherence more comprehensively in education (Fullan & Quinn, 2016).

Defining Coherence Making

Coherence is not alignment. The latter consists of the rational organization and explanation as to what the main pieces of the organization are and how they relate to each other: vision, goals, strategies, finances, accountability, training, and so on. If we addressed all of this rationally, it would bring us back to Morieux and Tollman's artificial complicatedness. Think of it this way:

- Alignment is rational.
- Coherence is emotional.

Rational explanations are less sticky—you have to memorize them. On the other hand, things you experience usually affect your emotions and stay with you. Thus, you must "experience" coherence. Our formal definition of coherence is:

> The shared depth of understanding about the purpose and nature of the work. (Fullan & Quinn, 2016, p. 1)

I ask the reader to dwell on the definition. "Shared depth" is not something you can get from as document, a rousing speech, or even as good professional learning experience. I only know one way to develop "shared, collective understanding," and that is through purposeful, day-to-day interaction. Coherence making is a cultural phenomenon. It is what you experience on a daily basis in the setting in which you work. If the collective culture is weak, there will be little retained learning. If it has the strength of collaborative professionalism, as we saw in Chapter 4, it has the ingredients for coherence making, as measured by the shared depth of understanding of the work and its outcomes. Learning in a culture of change includes learning deeply about the work as a group.

Our full Coherence Framework for Education is displayed in Figure 6.1, which is our attempt at avoiding clutter or making the complex too complicated. The framework has only four main components, yet it is comprehensive (i.e., covers the waterfront). It is also mutually exclusive (concepts don't overlap) and succinct (only four big pieces). We have discussed all of these elements across the chapters, so we can be brief here. Focusing direction is essentially about moral purpose,

Figure 6.1. The Coherence Framework for Education.

which is raising the bar and closing the gap for all students. We have added two critical elements to this definition. One is that we must consider clarity of strategy from the beginning of the process. Moral purpose does not go very far if it is not purposefully activated, as we discussed in Chapter 2. Second, as a result of our deep learning work we have widened the definition of moral purpose. At first it tended to be confined to literacy, numeracy, and high school graduation. After delving into Chapter 5, we see it as a matter of being "good at learning" and "good at life" (connectedness, and well-being)—see Quinn, McEachen, Fullan, Gardner, & Drummy (2020).

Moral purpose is dynamically related to collaborative cultures. One could say that you cannot develop solid moral purpose in the absence of collaboration, which should be clear from our discussion of the nine insights into the change process (Chapter 3). In collaborative cultures, moral purpose is jointly determined by leaders and members through focused work.

Third, deep learning is essential for giving coherence substance. Content is crucial here. Finally, securing accountability is built into our model because it becomes part of the culture—literally a culture of accountability that is part and parcel of the work.

We also do not see the Coherence Framework as step by step. It is like a pulsating heart; when all four chambers are operating, the organization is healthy. In some ways, quadrants 1 and 2 can be thought of as going together. You can't really focus direction without interacting with others. Focusing direction means you should select a small number of ambitious goals (a maximum of three). Developing collaborative cultures is hard because in involves changing culture—the daily habits of people. In Chapter 4, we saw how specific and persistent the actions must be, and how peers must be part and parcel of changing culture. Deep learning (Chapter 5) represents another cultural change, literally changing the nature of schooling as we know it. Quadrant four requires integrating a new culture of accountability.

Coherence making is complex, but I hope the agenda is clear. Leadership is crucial, as we will take up in the next chapter. Basically, leaders need to be "coherence makers." I can also note that coherence making is never completed. People come and go. Coherent systems have lower turnover of staff (because they are better places to work), but all organizations have turnover if you take any two or three years. Second, the environment changes—new policies and different political and demographic forces enter for better or worse. Third, hopefully you and your colleagues have new ideas along the way. All of these changes present additional coherence-making propositions. Coherent organizations have a more stable base, but they still must establish coherence making as an ongoing capacity.

Readers tell us that the Coherence Framework and its details are clear. We have 33 protocols aligned to support implementation (Fullan, Quinn, & Adam, 2016). People read the book, many times in study groups, and go away to implement the solution. Then they return and ask us, "How do you implement this stuff?" This involves another dimension of the change process: the nine change capacities in Chapter 2, for example. Change requires leadership that puts in the time to understand and work in each context, because each context in some respects is unique—a point we will return to in the next chapter.

In the meantime, if you appreciate that coherence is core, that you can only get it through thoughtful shared, purposeful interaction, and you must attend to it at all times—if you and your colleagues do all of these things daily, then you are in the game.

In effect, Chapter 4 on collaborative cultures addresses coherence in the individual organization. Recall Collins's flywheel effect when the interactive factors—such as passionate individuals, collaborative teams, good data, and so forth—generate ongoing focus.

Here I want to add to the challenge, "How do you achieve coherence when there are multiple subparts?" For example, the Toronto District School Board has 100 branch plants, or

583 schools. This takes us to our bigger "system coherence" framework that we call "leadership from the middle."

Leadership from the Middle

When we shift our lens to the system level—multiple levels and units—the matter of coherence obviously becomes more difficult. In system change—let's say the whole organization assuming multiple units—there are at least three levels: top management, middle management, and individual local units. In education, for example, this includes, respectively, state level, districts, and local schools.

After years of attempts at whole system change, we know that top-down change doesn't work (too complex, too much turnover, people don't follow orders). We also know that bottom-up change is not the answer (too many ad hoc pieces and uneven development). New Zealand, for example, in 1989 established a radical new plan called "Tomorrow's Schools," where each one of its 2,500 or so schools became autonomous with its own local board of governors. Over the ensuing decades, the gap between schools doing well or poor became significantly greater. In 2018, a new government established a new "Tomorrow's Schools Task Force" whose focus is how to coordinate schools to work together. It is still not determined what the solution will be, but hopefully ideas in leading in a culture of change will find a place.

If top-down doesn't work and bottom-up fails, where is the glue? We find it *in the middle*! Hargreaves and Shirley (2018) first surfaced this finding when they studied an initiative in Ontario, where the government funded a consortium of districts to implement a special education initiative.

They found great cooperation across districts, innovations that had support, and results that the districts collectively had caused.

Our team has since developed "leadership from the middle" (LftM) as a major component of our system strategy. We are using LftM, for example, to guide and interpret the reforms in California. The government over the past six years has developed a radical new system transformation called the California Way (Fullan, Rincón-Gallardo, & Gallagher, 2019). Its goal is to achieve success for all students in the state in terms of measurable results in excellence and equity. There are 1,009 local districts and 58 counties, about 12,000 regular and charter schools, and more than 6 million students. Overseeing the system there is the governor, a state superintendent of public instruction (an elected position), the California Department of Education (CDE), and several other agencies.

When we introduced LftM into the California system, educators and others by and large loved it (not to say that implementation is smooth). The reason that LftM has appeal is that those in the middle find that they have a proactive role. My image of the traditional middle is that the top tells them what to do, while the bottom complains that they are doing it. In LftM, the middle becomes a system resource. In the case of California, the middle are districts and counties. The solution requires districts and counties to work more closely together locally (vertically so to speak), and laterally across districts and counties—and for all of these to work more closely with CDE and related agencies. After six years, progress is being made, with crucial next steps before them (see Fullan, Rincón-Gallardo & Gallagher, 2019).

Our formal definition of the middle is:

A strategy that increases the capacity of the middle as it becomes a better partner laterally, upward and downward.

Most groups instantly find LftM appealing. As I said, the vast middle immediately sees a potentially new positive role for them. We have encountered many people in higher education and in K–12 systems that start using LftM thinking right away. We are also using LftM with several systems around the world: California, Victoria, Australia, and in our Deep Learning initiatives such as in Uruguay (see Quinn et al., 2020).

These various applications have led to further development and thinking about system change. Figure 6.2 represents our latest thinking.

Apologies for the slick jargon, but the essence of Figure 6.2 is:

- The top shapes the direction, invests, interacts, monitors direction, and proactively liberates downward.

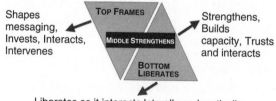

Figure 6.2.   General principles.

- The middle increases its capacity, interacts laterally within the middle, exploits upward, proactively liberates downward, and demonstrates accountability.

- The bottom exploits upward, interacts laterally, and demonstrates accountability.

A few words require explanation. Although it is oddly put, *exploit upwardly* is the correct concept for system change. Levels below the top should not want to find themselves constantly on the receiving end of top-down polices. By exploit, I mean that the lower levels proactively take into account and act on government policies relative to local priorities. In a word, they exploit polices in relation to local priorities. *Liberate those below you* means that you want to free "groups" to act on policies with some degree of freedom. When individuals are free, they act randomly; when groups are free, there are checks and balances that combine autonomy and collaboration (see my discussion in Chapter 4).

If you ask, "Where is the glue (the accountability)?" the answer is that it is in the combination of the focuses and the purposeful *interaction*. Yes, continuous interaction vertically and horizontally about progress serves the accountability function better than traditional accountability. Transparent and focused interaction sorts out what is working and what is not. *Note:* There are still the measures of progress, but they operative in a more interactive, supportive climate.

Independent from us, Morieux and Tollman (2014)—the "manage complexity without getting too complicated" authors—arrived at the same conclusions. They call one of their recommendations "increase reciprocity" that includes the concept *multiplexity* (networks of interaction). Leading in a culture of change means increasing the capacity of individuals and groups to make better decisions and engage in corresponding actions. It is purposeful interaction on a daily basis that feeds such capacity. In effect, Morieux and Tollman argue that such interactions "create feedback loops that expose people, as directly as possible to the consequences of their actions" (p. 110).

Multiplexity, say the authors, consists of "creating networks of interaction." Basically this takes us back to the collaborative cultures we discussed in Chapter 4. Teams doing the work get together regularly to review how things are going. Sometimes, this involves a given team examining its own work; other times teams compare notes, or engage in cross-visitations to learn from each other.

Morieux and Tollman conclude, as I do, that focused interaction—learning is the work—produces "greater accountability, less complicatedness" (p. 133). The objectives are ambitious combined with transparent actions and feedback that allow for corrective action:

> These feedback loops allow for decentralized control, since it is based on the interaction among people, each one partly controlling the behavior of others. Control becomes distributed and flexible, as opposed to top down and rigid, which enables the organization to be more adaptive to changing conditions. (p. 134)

In pursuing leadership from the middle, we also acknowledge that many efforts at change are ad hoc and piecemeal in business and in education. I mentioned in Chapter 4 my work with Laura Schwalm, the former superintendent of Garden Grove Unified School District in Anaheim, California. As we do our current work in the state to increase the collective focus of districts improving learning for all students, we encounter the tendency to take on ad hoc initiatives that, by definition, undermine coherence. In the rush to solutions, people inevitably operate more superficially. To counter this problem, we compiled a simple guideline that we called "Getting Serious about Getting Serious" (Figure 6.3).

We see in Figure 6.3 that each of the 10 items are strong in their own right, and they operate as a cluster of mutually reinforcing factors that constitute a *system* that transforms the culture of learning. You will also see that our set of "getting serious" elements compares favorably with Susan Moore Johnson's (2019) account of schools "where teachers thrive" that I described in Chapter 4. The difference is one of scale. Most of the examples of success in Chapter 4 deal with individual schools, whereas my work with Schwalm is about entire school districts—system with 40 or more schools, for example.

In any case, leadership from the middle is a coherence maker for systems. Coherence making is an integral part of our model, as it serves to bring together moral purpose, new insights about the change process, and knowledge.

We have pursued system change more systematically in a new study where we examined the roles and relationships across three levels: local, middle and top in a book with the tantalizing title: The Devil is in the details: System solutions for equity, excellence and wellbeing (Fullan & Gallagher (2020).

Getting Serious about Getting Serious

Laura Schwalm and Michael Fullan
January 2019

For those who believe a school system cannot be better than its teachers and understand that if teachers are expected to thoughtfully build student capacity, the same thought must be given to teacher capacity building. We hope these scenarios will provoke your thinking.

Scenario A:
A system *very serious* about capacity building

Scenario B:
A system *not serious* about capacity building

1. Has a rigorous systemwide selection process and criteria for selecting new teachers. Selects for collaborative skills and commitment to ongoing learning.

1. Does not have a system with standards for hiring new teachers and simply selects from the applications they have on hand.

2. Sees teachers as the solution and supports them to develop individual and collective efficacy.

2. Sees teachers as the problem and tries to fix them as individuals.

3. Understands that great teaching is extremely difficult and demanding and takes years to master through working collaboratively with others.

3. Assumes that teaching is not a highly skilled profession and can be fairly quickly trained in individuals.

4. Thoughtfully explores (with principals and teachers) the reasons behind lack of student achievement in targeted areas before jumping to solutions.

4. Schedules trainings based on the problems you perceive teachers, and thus students, are having and assumes that more training in that area will fix them.

5. Understands that no matter how good the professional development session(s) are, it takes practice to improve skills (great teaching takes great skill), so unless the sessions are followed up with support as the teachers try to implement what they learned, strong results will be unlikely.

5. Assumes that if the trainings are done well, the teachers should know what to do, or it is the principals' job to help them and see that it gets done.

Figure 6.3.   Getting Serious about Getting Serious.

6. Draws on both internal and external expertise to build capacity.	6. Relies on the latest and greatest Sage on the Stage.
7. Supports professional development with appropriate tools and materials.	7. Expects teachers to make do with the materials and tools they already have, or to develop or purchase their own.
8. Recognizes that both content knowledge and strong pedagogy are important and includes both in professional development plans.	8. Neglects the importance of strong pedagogy and assumes that all teachers need is to know more about math or …
9. Believes that teachers are the most important (and largest expenditure in the budget) and thus, tending to that investment is essential.	9. Teacher support and capacity building is viewed as important but not essential.
10. Cultivates innovation with staff and students to strengthen student learning and wellbeing and achieve equity for all.	10. Stays with academic learning as traditionally taught.

While the scenarios above are designed to provoke thinking about how to build and sustain strong professional capacity building for teachers, training and coaching alone will not make a great teacher. The importance of hiring practices that yield teachers who have naturally high expectations for all students, combined with true caring for their achievement and well-being, is critical. Suffice it to say that if you expect your teachers to truly care about all of their students, your teachers must feel that you have the same care and concern for them.

Figure 6.3. (*Continued*)

Conclusion

Remember from Figure 1.1 in Chapter 1 that the route to making more good things happen and preventing more bad things from occurring is a process that generates widespread internal commitment from members of the organization. When change occurs, there will be disturbances, and this means that there will be differences of opinion that must be reconciled. Effective leadership means guiding people through the differences and, indeed, making differences a source of new insights as they lead to more integrative and focused solutions . . . .

Working directly on coherence making is essential in a world that is loaded with uncertainty and confusion. But you do need to go about coherence making by honoring the change guidelines in previous chapters, which in effect require differences about the nature and direction of change to be identified and confronted. Rest assured, also, that the processes embedded in pursuing moral purpose, the change process, new relationships, and knowledge sharing do actually produce greater and deeper coherence as they unfold.

This is a time to emphasize that there is a great deal of coherence making in Figure 1.1 from start to finish. Moral purpose sets the context; it calls for people to aspire to greater accomplishments. The standards embedded in strong moral purpose in relation to outcomes can be very high indeed, as they are in the cases cited in this book.

This moral purpose–outcome combination won't work if we don't respect the messiness of the process required to identify best solutions and generate internal commitment from the majority of organization members. Within the apparent disorder of the process there are hidden coherence-making features. The first of these features is what can be called lateral accountability. In hierarchical systems, it is easy to get away with superficial compliance or even subtle sabotage. In the interactive system I have been describing, both good and bad work get noticed (or, more accurately, people recognize and sort out what is working). Over time, things that work get retained and what doesn't work gets discarded. This process is built into the culture of daily interaction.

We have come on a pretty complicated journey. I have said that leadership in a culture of change requires a new mind-set that serves as a guide to day-to-day organization development and performance. We obtained, I hope, a good sense of what the mind-set consists of and a good sense of how it plays itself out in actual cases from businesses and school systems.

Ideas about the new leadership required have been dispersed throughout the chapters. Also, the key leadership competencies have been implied rather than systematically considered. It is time to pull together more comprehensively what the new leadership looks like. Be prepared. It is different from what we might have assumed. It is, as you might have inferred, more dynamic, less linear, and, in a word, more nuanced.

Chapter Seven

Leadership for Change

I N AESOP'S FABLE, THE TORTOISE AND THE HARE, THE
hare is quick, clever, high on hubris, and a loser. The tortoise is slow and purposeful; it adapts to the terrain and is a winner. The lesson is very close to my own adage: "Go slow to go fast." The beginning is very important. Going fast can miss context and fail to connect people to their issues and their potential. Too quick and you miss vital learning. Just right and you create accelerating momentum.

There is a difference in my model since the leaders are not exactly tortoise-like. In given change situations, if you lead effectively (as in a culture of change), you gain momentum as you go because more and more people are on board, and they have great specificity and shared coherence. Go slow to go fast, as we call it. I do believe that we can accomplish greater change in shorter periods of time if we understand what it means to lead in a culture of change. Thus, we need to dig deeper into what effective leadership looks like in these complex times.

In this chapter, I begin with the observation that overall, *leadership is a mess,* not at all up to the challenge of leading effectively in a culture of dynamic and complex change. Then I turn to a threefold framework: appointing leaders; learning as you go; and leaving a legacy.

Leadership Is a Mess

We can start with the widespread finding that almost two-thirds of employees on the average are not actively engaged in their organizations (see Chapter 2). This applies to teachers and students as well as members of most organizations. It is slightly unfair to call this a "leadership problem" but it is. If not the fault of individual leaders, it is the failure of organizations to position leadership effectively. It is accurate to conclude that leadership has not yet found its niche in leading dynamic complex systems.

Recall from the Gallup review in Chapter 2 that the single biggest factor in the performance of individuals and teams is the quality of management. The problem starts with the hiring and appointment of leaders. Peter Cappelli (2019) from the Wharton School in Philadelphia completed a review and titled his report "Your Approach to Hiring Is All Wrong." He found only a third of companies check whether their recruitment process produces good employees. There is now a tendency to hire from outside. Up until the 1970s, 90% of leadership vacancies came from inside the company. Today, according to Cappelli, barely a third hire from within. Outside hiring has more unknowns—at least in terms of how organizations go about it. It is often outsourced to headhunters; it depends too much on interviews that are notoriously open to bias; it doesn't get at past performance; and it takes longer for outsiders to get up to speed. Selection techniques, concludes Cappelli, "are a bit of a mess."

We also saw in Chapter 1 Chamorro-Premuzic's (2019) findings that 75% of workers who quit their job do so because of their direct line manager (p. 1). He concludes that "most leaders are bad" and that we overvalue "confidence and assertiveness" (p. 12). He also makes the case for hiring more women, which is another matter. The point is that we often appoint leaders for superficial reasons because they look and sound good, not necessarily whether they can do good.

I did a small, informal test in June 2019 via my Twitter account, where I have 51,000 followers. This is by no means a scientific study (for one thing people who have bad bosses would be unlikely to say so on Twitter). My questions was, "What percentage of leaders are good as in focusing the agenda, working alongside others to get results, and having a positive impact on the organizations?" Incidentally, I think it is difficult under conditions of growing complexity to be this effective. But that is the point. We need especially good leaders to lead cultures of change, and if anything we are not being careful in the recruitment and cultivation of leaders.

Personally, I had predicted that around 20% of leaders would be considered to be highly effective. Within a week, I received 136 replies. Here are some of them:

- 20%, being optimistic.
- 10%—so sad.

- 90% mean well; only 45% truly engage the group.

- In my 20 years of teaching: 1 in 20.

- Less than 10%; the rest think they are—just ask them.

- 95% best intentions; but would guess it is really about 25%.

- At best 7%. The rest are maintaining the status quo with only incremental changes and calling them innovations.

- It doesn't look good—20%. Keep in mind it's a tough gig.

- 30% with a crisis brewing.

The modal response was in the 5–30% range; a handful of responders estimated 65% or so.

Speaking of Twitter, my good colleague Terry Grier, who was the brilliant superintendent of the large, complex, and successful Houston Independent School District, had this to say on June 16, 2019. I think he was lamenting that there were too many bad choices when he offered:

> When selecting leaders, how do you identify 'the real deal'?
> Ask additional questions tied to your organizational goals;
> ask probing questions to people NOT listed as references;
> and monitor once hired; replace a bad hire as quickly as
> possible—don't wait until year's end!

All and all, my point is not just that there are bad or ineffective leaders, but more that leading in a culture of change is more complex than recognized. To put it another way, leading in systems of growing complexity requires another level of leadership than was hitherto required.

In the rest of this chapter, I first examine the new complexity of leadership including my newest findings about *Nuance*. I then conclude with what it takes to become highly effective, that is, how do the best leaders actually get that good.

Lessons for Leading in a Culture of Change

There is no question that the environment is changing at an accelerating rate. Under these conditions, it is understandable that some leaders want to match speed with speed. If you go fast and it is superficial, you end up spinning your wheels. Typically, people get left behind. What looks like fast change is an illusion. It feels hectic, but there is little substance.

Change has changed. It is more dynamic with many more opportunities—to fail as well as to succeed. If I distill the lessons in this book, they come down to saying that leadership needs to change because the situation has changed in irreversible ways. Essentially, leadership must become less linear without losing focus.

Heifetz and Linsky (2017) capture the nature of this new leadership work as they expand on the difference between "technical and adaptive work." Technical change is when the problem is straightforward and requires the use of existing knowledge to address it. In this case, people look to proven experts to solve the problem. The authors then say that almost all of our problems (and they are growing in number and difficulty) require "adaptive solutions."

The leadership challenge is very different for adaptive problems as they express:

> For transformative change to be sustainable it not only has to take root in its own culture, but also has to successfully engage its changing environment. It must be adaptive to both internal and external realities. Therefore, leadership needs to start by listening and learning, finding out where people are, valuing what is best in what they already know, and do, and build from there. (Heifetz & Linsky, 2017, p. xiv)

To continue with the spirit of this new leadership, I reproduce in Figure 7.1 a diagram we use in workshops when we are training people in the new leadership.

One can readily see how this sequence of learning and development maps onto Heifetz and Linsky's conclusions about the need for adaptive (but nonetheless focused) leadership.

Let's also examine the new leadership as a list of traits or characteristics as in Figure 7.2.

Figure 7.1. New leadership.

1. Be a lead learner from day one.
2. Listen and learn.
3. Be an expert and an apprentice.
4. Learn in context.
5. Make your moral compass dynamic.
6. Make yourself dispensable (in the right way).

Figure 7.2. Leadership for change.

I turn first to my new study of "nuanced" leaders (who are essentially like those depicted in Figure 7.1). You may recall Marie-Claire Bretherton from Chapter 2, who was appointed as the new principalship of an absolutely terrible school in northern England that had been stuck near the bottom of performance for a decade. It was obvious "what" needed to be changed, but not "how." Instead of jumping into changes right away, Marie-Claire did two things. She interviewed all staff from cleaners to deputy head. Then she and her assistant, Sam, went on a learning mission.

> Myself and Sam had a policy. For the first 8 weeks we would not give any feedback. We literally went on a mission to find anything that we could possibly observe that was good. (Fullan, 2019, p. 17)

Within 18 months the school went from being a failing disaster to winning an award for school of the year—a clear example of go slow to go fast.

Similarly, how could John Malloy go about making progress in the Toronto District School Board (TDSB) with its 583 schools when he was appointed director in January 2016. He talks about the starting point: "I inherited a culture that when you talk about system direction, people then start expecting the templates, the recipes and the roadmaps" (Fullan, 2019, p. 51).

John then restructured the local subsystem to create 28 clusters of 20 schools each (compared to the previous 20 clusters of 30 schools). He then set up a system where he accompanied his 28 area superintendents on school visits throughout the year in order to learn more about the schools and what they might need, and notably to model with the area superintendents what lead learners should do on a daily basis. John, too, was a leader and learner from day one.

In both cases, Bretherton and Malloy were lead learners from the get-go. They were trying to make meaning in the system. At the beginning they had more questions than answers, then they learned more and more. Time and again in cases of success we see leaders "participate as learners" with teachers, principals, and others as they move schools and the system forward.

Such leaders blend and integrate qualities 1 and 2 in Figure 7.2. They are role models for their systems. They learn deeply about the culture and the people through such immersion. At first they have more questions than answers. They listen and listen and then they learn and learn. Before long they learn things perhaps more than others in the system as they cut across the schools. Their questions and suggestions become more informed.

I thank my colleague Roger Martin and fellow researcher Sally Osberg for our third revelation in Figure 7.2. In their study of social entrepreneurship in developing countries where the worlds of the expert and the roles of those living in the situation were vastly different, Martin and Osberg

(2015) found that both groups were sources of expertise, knowledge, and insights.

Expert knowledge in a given domain is only one part of the solution, note Martin and Osberg. Effective leaders learn to draw on the wisdom of those not seen or classified as "experts." Leaders need to position themselves "to absorb lessons from ecosystem actors, especially those disadvantaged by the existing equilibrium" (p. 92). Leaders in a culture of change are not afraid to display their knowledge about things they know (even then they are ready to learn), but they are also hungry to learn when it comes to areas about which they are less knowledgeable. I learned this as well about nuanced leaders. They were relentlessly committed to solving problems, but they were also humble when it came to things they did not know.

Fourth, we have encountered several times in this book the new finding (it should have been obvious) that lead learners always become knowledgeable about the context in which they work. My colleague and fellow consultant, Brendan Spillane, defines nuance as "action informed by deep contextual literacy" (personal communication). All if the elements in Figure 7.2 feed into this notion.

A corollary of "learn in context" is another new finding. Every time you go to a new context, such as change jobs as a leader, you automatically become *deskilled* in relation to new context. Acting in the manner of expert and apprentice in a new situation is a winning combination. Of course you learn more each time so it accumulates. I would venture to say, given our discussion of ineffective leadership in Chapter 1, that many a leader does not learn deeply within their own cultures even though they may have been on the job for a decade or more. It is all about fashioning yourself as a learner, but also not being afraid to be assertive when the situation calls for it. If it is clear that you are a learner, people will welcome your decisiveness when it is needed.

Fifth, making your moral compass dynamic or active means that your moral values and commitments must be evident to all. Remember the LRN study in Chapter 1 that observable moral purpose on the part of senior management was absent in the eyes of most employees. The consequence:

> When CEOs do not consistently behave as moral leaders, 89% of managers under them fail to lead with moral authority. (LRN, 2019, p. 5)

Recall that moral leadership was based on letting purpose lead, inspiring others, animating values and virtues, and building and keeping the moral agenda front and center.

The sixth and final attribute is revealing. Basically, it says that your job as a leader is to spend six or seven years or so developing a collaborative culture of leadership to the point where you become "dispensable." If you don't leave a legacy culture of the kind we have been discussing in this book you will have failed as a leader. When you do all the things in Figure 7.2 you are de facto a mentor for your organization. You can do other things such as being more aware of and attentive to the kind of human and social talent needed in the organization, establish formal mentoring programs, promote the culture we have been discussing in this book, and being more proactive and explicit about the culture you are cultivating with others.

How Do Highly Effective Leaders Become So Good?

In this book we have examined the five main dimensions of leading in a culture of change: moral purpose, understanding change, relationships, knowledge creation and use, and coherence making. We saw that ineffective leaders often have high degrees of confidence and assertiveness. The deeper aspects of effective leadership require the would-be leader to put in the time to learn them as he or she gets better and better each step of the way. The good news is that good leadership accelerates because by definition you are learning daily.

To capture the nature and spirit of getting better at complex endeavors, I turn to Anders Ericsson, the researcher that Malcolm Gladwell made famous by citing the 10,000-hour rule that states that anybody can become an expert if they put in the 10,000 hours of practice. Ericsson and Pool (2016) wrote the definitive book partly to set the record straight. It turns out that what makes the difference is 10,000 hours of *cumulative deliberate practice.*

Long a tenet of our approach, this is the idea that you get better at something by doing the work itself with a purposeful practice mindset. Ericsson says that such practice has four characteristics:

1. It has well-defined, specific goals.
2. It is focused.
3. It involves feedback.
4. It requires getting out of one's comfort zone (Ericsson & Pool, pp. 15–17).

For leadership Ericsson notes, "Our starting point is the measurement of performance in the real world" (personal communication, April 2016).

In every case of expert performance, leaders become much better at what Ericsson calls "mental representations" of the situation at hand. The good news is that almost all of us can get better over time through deliberate practice:

> The main thing that sets experts apart from the rest of us is that their years if experience have changed the neural circuitry in the brain to produce highly specialized mental representations, which in turn makes possible the incredible memory pattern recognition, problem solving, and other sorts of advanced abilities needed to excel in their particular specialties. (p. 46)

If we examine two of our most accomplished "nuanced" leaders—Marie-Clare Bretherton and John Malloy—you will see the development of this expertise at work (Fullan, 2019). They both have a strong sense of moral direction. They are committed to making a difference. But at the early stages they did not know "how" to do this. They saw it as essential that they needed to figure it out by getting inside the problem as a learner. They were willing to get outside their comfort zones. They become clearer and more committed through the work.

After a while, they developed greater insights. It seems that their sense of intuition increased. I would say that this was not because they were born with greater intuition but, rather, that increased intuition is derived from their experiences of taking on more difficult challenges (outside their comfort zones, to quote Ericsson).

All of this is very much compatible with the discoveries about nuance. Nuance leaders immerse themselves in context because they know that context is crucial. They build relationships and get insights with the people they are leading. Each new context, as I said before, to a certain extent "de-skills leaders"—because you need to learn the details and nuances of the new context in order to be effective in it. But it gets easier as you go from context to context for two reasons. First, you know that becoming context-literate is essential so you become oriented and committed to learning about each new context. Second, you start to recognize patterns, and therefore you see patterns more readily.

Nuance revealed another insight about one of the most elusive concepts in leadership, namely *courage*. Observers of leadership have always touted "courage" but it came across as you either have it or not. Now we see something more subtle. Our effective leaders certainly have a strong moral compass. Then, through attempting more and more and being successful, they actually become *more courageous.* Marie-Claire Bretherton put it this way: "I think I have probably underestimated in the past the power of your own sense of vision and hope, and your own mental discipline, and your own belief" (Fullan, 2019, p. 41).

This conclusion about the role of courage in leadership—it is a product of action (and then becomes a greater force in its own right)—is corroborated by Povey and McInerney's (2019) book, *The Leadership Factor.* They identify six Cs as leadership factors: curiosity, changeability, charisma, connection, collaboration, and courage (mostly these are compatible with what I have been saying, although "charisma" would be questionable in my model). Povey and McInerney conclude that "courage" develops as a result of working on the other six factors. The "how" of developing courage is to immerse oneself with others in trying to change something significant, using the skills that I have been addressing in this book, and becoming more courageous as a result of your experiences, skill development, and accomplishments. As I concluded in *Nuance*, such leaders become courageously and relentlessly committed to a better future. They maintain their humility and empathy, but are passionately loyal to achieving with others a better future that improves humanity (Fullan, 2019, p. 112).

Nuanced leaders—leaders in a culture of change—see the bigger picture; they don't panic when things go wrong in the early stages of a major change initiative. It is not so much that they take their time, but rather that they know it takes time for things to gel. In a sense, they establish the conditions for change and become increasingly persistent about progress.

All through this book the message has been that organizations transform when they can establish mechanisms for learning in the dailiness of organizational life. As Elmore (2000) stated:

> People make … fundamental transitions by having many opportunities to be exposed to ideas, to argue them to their own normative belief systems, to practice the behaviors that go with those values, to observe others practicing those behaviors, and, most importantly, to be successful at practicing in the presence of others (that is, to be seen to be successful). In the panoply of rewards and sanctions that attach to accountability systems, the most powerful incentives reside in the face-to-face relationships among people in the organization, not in external systems. (p. 31)

When Henry Mintzberg was asked what organizations have to do to ensure success over the next 10 years, he responded:

> They've got to build a strong core of people who really care about the place and who have ideas. Those ideas have to flow freely and easily through the organization. It's not a question of riding in with a great new chief executive on a great white horse. Because as soon as that person rides out, the whole thing collapses unless somebody can do it again. So it's a question of building strong institutions, not creating heroic leaders. Heroic leaders get in the way of strong institutions. (quoted in Bernhut, 2000, p. 23)

Strong institutions have many leaders at all levels. Those in a position to be leaders of leaders, such as the CEO, know that they do not run the place. They know that they are cultivating leadership in others, and they realize that they are doing more than planning for their own succession—that if they "lead right," the organization will outgrow them. Thus, the ultimate leadership contribution is to develop leaders in the organization who can move the organization even further after they have left (see Lewin & Regine, 2000, p. 220).

I feel compelled to argue again that the main message of this book is not to develop better individual leaders. Rather, the key point is to develop and foster better leadership cultures. We know that this is going to be enormously difficult for two reasons. The first is that the incentives seem to favor hiring what appear to be confident, articulate individuals—what Chamorro-Premuzic (2019) called "confidence disguised as competence" (Chapter 2). We can't get there (leadership cultures) from here (hiring overconfident individuals).

There is certainly a bias in the literature favoring human capital, or individual heroism—a problem recently stressed by Jonathan Aldred (2019) in a new book titled *Licence to Be Bad: How Economics Corrupted Us*. Economists, argues Aldred, take a narrow view of humans as selfish creatures. Alfred likely overstates the case, but even if humans are not as self-centered calculators as he claims, he is likely right that we do not have enough social learning and collective efficacy in our institutions. I also referred in Chapter 4 to the $575 million multiyear effort undertaken by the Bill & Melinda Gates Foundation to increase (individual) teacher effectiveness, which failed to make a difference because it focused mainly on the individual teacher (Stecher et al., 2018).

The good news in "leading in a culture of change" is that people rise to the occasion when they are helped by leaders who develop others to do something that is individually and collectively worthwhile. Such leaders tap into fundamental virtues of humans—and when they do, improvement happens quickly.

One of the main conclusions I have drawn is that the requirements of knowledge societies bring education and business leadership closer than they have ever been before. Corporations need souls and schools need minds (of course they need both) if the knowledge society is to survive—sustainability demands it. New mutual respect and part-nerships between the corporate and education worlds are needed, especially concerning leadership development. Such endeavors must be based on and guided by the forces discussed in Chapters 2 through 6.

Recent conclusions by evolutionary biologists have placed new more dramatic spotlights on the crucial state of human and moral purpose as we complete the first fifth of the twenty-first century. There is little doubt that the world is becoming more troubled: climate change, unknown future of jobs and the economy; dramatically increasing inequity across the world (the discrepancy between the haves and the have nots), increased stress and anxiety across all groups, unintended consequences of technology including more impersonal connections, decrease in trust, and ultimately threats to global social cohesion.

What do the evolutionary biologist have to say about the trends? I referred to this earlier. The argument is complex, but not difficult to amass (see especially Wilson, 2014; Wilson, 2019, and neuroscientist, Antonio Damasio, 2018, p. 2). Here are some of the key conclusions:

1. *Humans are not intrinsically good.* Each of us is conflicted; sometimes selfish, other times committing to others and the common good (only sociopaths—1% or so of the population—are oblivious to good).

2. *We are social beings (born to connect).* "The inherited propensities to communicate, recognize and evaluate, bond cooperate, compete, and from all these, the deep warm pleasure of belonging to our own special group" (Edward, O. Wilson, p. 75). BUT, this can just as easily take the form of "tribalism"—my group good; all others bad or irrelevant.

3. *Goodness can evolve.* Building on (2), David Sloan Wilson states: "Modern evolutionary theory tells us that goodness *can* evolve, but only when special

conditions are met. That's why we must become wise managers of evolutionary processes. Otherwise evolution takes us where we don't want to go" (pp. 13–14).

4. *We are a population of groups.* "This means that an evolving population is not just a population of individuals, but also a population of *groups*. If individuals vary in their propensity for good and evil, then this variation will exist at two levels: variation among individuals within groups, and variation among groups within the entire population" (David Sloan Wilson, p. 77).

5. *Forming harmonious groups is becoming more challenging.* Damasio argues that in simpler times, things turned out well because our instincts to form groups and to achieve levels of harmony eventually prevailed. Now, says Damasio, given our more complex evolution and the troubling challenges we face, things may become radically different: "To expect *spontaneous* homeostatic harmony from large and cacophonous human collectives is to expect the unlikely" (p. 219, italics in original).

These potential developments raise moral purpose to a whole new level—the survival of humankind and the planet itself! We already know that engagement and satisfaction with work and life is on the wane in most organizations, businesses, or schools alike. Now we have one more compelling reason to pay heed—survival itself. But there is more than this. Leading in a culture of change is about fulfillment and flourishing.

When you strip away all the layers, "leading in a culture of change" is about human fulfillment. Why are we on this earth? There is no answer really, but the notion of creating things individually and collectively beyond our imagination, and then some—let's call it the Leonardo da Vinci factor—is not a bad aspiration. This is where Edward O. Wilson ends up going. His solution is to combine a greater respect for the mysteries and ideas within evolutionary biology with the creative freedom of the humanities: "The creative arts for their part continued to flower with brilliant and idiosyncratic expressions of the human imagination" (p. 39).

We can ground this even more. Yes, worry about survival. And at the same time, develop the profound strengths of our fivefold solution: pursue moral purpose, understand change dynamics, establish multiple focused relationships, probe the depths of knowledge creation, and work on the dynamics of coherence-making.

Conclusion

Within all of this is the realization that business, education, governments, and the variety of other agencies have something in common: the moral purpose of living in a dynamic, exciting, and admittedly dangerous world.

The closeness of business and education entities has been further reinforced by our work on "Deep Learning." The focus on the 6Cs (character, citizenship, collaboration, communication, creativity, and critical thinking), and the link to the theme of "Engage the world, Change the world" provides a common and urgent agenda (Fullan, Quinn, & McEachen, 2018; Quinn, McEachen, Fullan, Gardner and

Drummy, 2020). The world is currently going down an extremely challenging path—one that calls for urgent, joint action that has leading in a culture of change as its common theme of salvation and flourishing.

As world problems continuously emerge and show up at our doorstep, and as we experience the virtues and uplifting impact of leaders who know how to lead and shape cultures of change we may, just may, see a rise in the quality of leadership, which at the current time is woefully weak.

David Sloan Wilson observed that "goodness *can* evolve, but only when special conditions are met." One of these special conditions is the development of "leadership for and within cultures of change." Ultimately, your leadership in a culture of change will be judged as effective or ineffective not just by who you are as a leader but by what leadership you produce in others. There is no time to waste.

References

Aldred, J. (2019). *Licence to be bad: How economics corrupted us*. London, UK: Allemn Lane.

Argyris, C. (2000). *Flawed advice and the management trap*. New York, NY: Oxford University Press.

Beer, M., Eisenstat, R., & Spector, B. (1990). *The critical path to corporate renewal*. Boston, MA: Harvard Business School Press.

Bernhut, S. (2000, September-October). Henry Mintzberg in conversation. *Ivey Business Journal*, 19–23.

Bernstein, P. (1996). *Against the gods*. New York, NY: Wiley.

Bishop, B. (2000). *The strategic enterprise*. Toronto, Ontario: Stoddart.

Bishop, R. (2019). *Teaching to the North-East: Realtionship-based learning in practice*. Wellington, NZ: New Zealand Council for Education Research.

Brown, J. S., & Duguid, P. (2000). *The social life of information*. Boston, MA: Harvard Business School Press.

Bryant, A. (2013). *Honeywell's David Cote on decisiveness as a two-edged sword.* New York Times. http:nytimes.com

Cappelli, P. (2019). Your approach to hiring is all wrong. *Harvard Business Review* (May–June).

Chamorro-Premuzic, T. (2019). *Why do so many incompetent men become leaders?* Boston, MA: Harvard Business Review Press.

Clifton, J., & Harter, J. (2019). *It's the manager.* New York, NY: Gallup Press.

Cole, P. (2004). *Professional development: A great day to avoid change.* Melbourne, AU: Centre for Strategic Education.

Collins, J. (2019). *Turning the flywheel: A monograph to accompany good to great.* New York, NY, Random House.

Damasio, A. (2018). *The strange order of things.* New York, NY: Pantheon Books.

Darrah, C. (1993). Workplace training, workplace learning: A case study. *Human Organization, 54*(1), 31–41.

Datnow, A., & Park, V. (2019). *Professional collaboration with purpose.* London, UK: Routledge.

Dixon, N. (2000). *Common knowledge.* Boston, MA: Harvard Business School Press.

Donohoo, J., Hattie, J., & Eells, R. (2018). The power of collective efficacy. *Education Leadership.*

Donohoo, J., & Katz, S. (2020). *Quality implementation.* Thousand Oaks, CA.: Corwin Press.

Elmore, R. F. (2000). *Building a new structure for school leadership.* Washington, DC: Albert Shanker Institute.

Elmore, R. F. (2004). *School reform from the inside out.* Cambridge, MA: Harvard University Press.

Elmore, R. F., & Burney, D. (1999). Investing in teacher learning: Staff development and instructional improvement. In L. Darling-Hammond & G. Sykes (Eds.), *Teaching as the learning profession: Handbook of policy and practice* (pp. 236–291). San Francisco, CA: Jossey-Bass.

Ericsson, A., & Pool, R. (2016). *Peak: Secrets from the new science of expertise*. New York, NY: Houghton Mifflin.

Fullan, M. (2001). *The new meaning of educational change* (3rd ed.). New York, NY: Teachers College Press.

Fullan, M. (2008). *The six secrets of change*. San Francisco, CA: Jossey-Bass.

Fullan, M. (2010). *Motion leadership: The skinny on becoming change savvy*. Thousand Oaks, CA: Corwin Press.

Fullan, M. (2011). *The moral imperative realized*. Thousand Oaks, CA: Corwin Press.

Fullan, M. (2014). *The principal: Three keys for maximizing impact*. San Francisco, CA: Jossey-Bass.

Fullan, M. (2017). *Indelible leadership: Always leave them learning*. Thousand Oaks, CA: Corwin Press.

Fullan, M. (2019). *Nuance: Why some leaders succeed and others fail*. Thousand Oaks, CA: Corwin Press.

Fullan, M. & Gallagher, M. J. (2020). *The devil is in the details: System solutions for equity, excellence, and wellbeing*. Thousand Oaks, CA: Corwin.

Fullan, M., Gardner, M., & Drummy, M. (2019). Going deeper. *Education Leadership*, (May), 64–68.

Fullan, M., & Hargreaves, A. (1992). *What's worth fighting for? Working together for your school*. Toronto, Ontario/New York, NY: Elementary Teachers Federation of Ontario/Teachers College Press.

Fullan, M., & Pinchot, M. (2018). *The fast track to sustainable turnaround*. Educational Leadership. V 75, 48–54.

Fullan, M., Quinn, J., & Adam, E. (2016). *Taking action guide to building coherence in schools, districts, and systems*. Thousand Oaks, CA: Corwin.

Fullan, M., & Quinn, J. (2015). *Coherence: The right drivers in action*. Thousand Oaks, CA: Corwin Press.

Fullan, M., Quinn, J., & McEachen, J. (2018). *Deep learning: Engage the world change the world*. Thousand Oaks, CA: Corwin Press.

Fullan, M., Rincón-Gallardo, S., & Gallagher, M.J. (2019). *Learning is the work*. www.michaelfullan.ca

Gittell, J. (2003). *The Southwest Airlines way*. New York, NY: McGraw-Hill.

Gleick, J. (1999). *Faster*. New York, NY: Pantheon Books.

Goffee, R., & Jones, G. (2000, September–October). Why should anyone be led by you? *Harvard Business Review*, 63–70.

Goleman, D. (2000). March-April. Leadership that gets results. *Harvard Business Review*, 78–90.

Google. (2019). *Project Aristotle*. Mountain View, CA: Google.

Grank, A., Hughes, J., & Hunter, P. D. (2006). *Building the best*. Toronto, Canada: VIKING.

Gwande, A. (2007). *Better: A surgeon's notes on performance*. New York, NY: Metropolitan Books.

Hamel, G. (2000). *Leading the revolution*. Boston: Harvard Business School Press.

Hargreaves, A., & O'Connor, M. (2018). *Collaborative professionalism*. Thousand Oaks, CA: Corwin Press.

Hargreaves, A., & Shirley, D. (2018). *Leading from the middle*. Toronto, Ontario: Ontario Council of Directors of Education.

Heifetz, R. (1994). *Leadership without easy answers*. Cambridge, MA: Harvard University Press.

Heifetz, R., & Linsky, M. (2017). *Leadership on the line*. Boston, MA: Harvard Business Review Press.

Herold, D., & Fedor, D. (2008). *Change: The way you lead change*. Stanford, CA: Stanford University Press.

Homer-Dixon, T. (2000). *The ingenuity gap*. Toronto, Canada: Knopf.

Isaacson, W. (2017). *Leonardo da Vinci*. New York, NY: Simon & Schuster.

Jenkins, L. (2013). *Permission to forget*. Milwaikee, WI: American Society for Quality Press.

Johnson, S. M. (2019). *Where teachers thrive: Organizing students for success*. Cambridge, MA: Harvard Education Press.

Kotter, J. (1996). *Leading change*. Boston, MA: Harvard Business School Press.

Lewin, R., & Regine, B. (2000). *The soul at work*. New York, NY: Simon & Schuster.

Liker, J., & Meier, D. (2007). *Toyota talent*. New York, NY: McGraw-Hill.

LRN. (2019). The state of moral leadership in business. www .howmetrics.com.

Martin, R., & Osberg, S. (2015). *Getting beyond better*. Boston, MA: Harvard Business Review Press.

McFee, A., & Brynjolfsson, E. (2017). *Harnessing the digital world*. New York: NY: W.W. Norton.

Mehta, J., & Fine, S. (2019). *In search of deeper learning*. Cambridge, MA: Harvard University Press.

Metropolitan Life Insurance Co. (2013). *The MetLife survey of the American teacher*. New York, NY: Author.

Micklethwait, J., & Wooldridge, A. (1996). *The witch doctors: Making sense of management gurus*. New York, NY: Random House.

Mintzberg, H. (2004). *Managers not MBAs*. San Francisco, CA: Berrett-Koehler.

Mintzberg, H., Ahlstrand, B., & Lampel, J. (1998). *Strategy safari: A guided tour through the wilds of strategic management*. New York, NY: Free Press.

Morieux, Y., & Tollman, P. (2014). *Six simple rules: How to manage complexity without getting complicated*. Boston, MA: Harvard Business Review Press.

Munby, S. (2019). *Imperfect leadership*. London, UK: Crown Publishing.

Niver, L. (2013). Why so many of America's teachers are leaving the profession. *Huffington Post*. November 5. https://www .huffpost.com/entry/teaching-profession_b_4172238

Nonaka, I., & Takeuchi, H. (1995). *The knowledge-creating company*. Oxford, UK: Oxford University Press.

Polyani, M. (1983). *The tacit dimension*. Gloucester, MA: Peter Smith.

Povey, D., & McInerney, L. (2019). *The leadership factor*. Melton, Woodbridge, UK: John Catt Education Ltd.

Quinn, J., McEachen, J., Fullan, M., Gardner, M., & Drummy, M. (2020). *Dive into deep learning: Tools for engagement*. Thousand Oaks, CA: Corwin Press.

Reeves, D. (2009). *Leading change in your school*. Alexandria, VA: Association of School Curriculum Development.

Reeves, D. (2019). *Finding your leadership focus*. New York, NY: Teachers College Press.

Ridley, M. (1996). *The origins of virtue*. Harmondsworth, UK: Penguin Books.

Ries, E. (2017). *The startup way*. New York. Currency Publishing.

Schein, E. (2010). *Organizational culture and leadership* (4th ed.). San Francisco, CA: Jossey-Bass.

Senge, P., Cambron-McCabe, N., Lucas, T., Smith, B., Dutton, J., & Kleiner, A. (2000). *Schools that learn*. New York, NY: Doubleday.

Sergiovanni, T. J. (1999). *The lifeworld of leadership: Creating culture, community, and personal meaning in our schools*. San Francisco, CA: Jossey-Bass.

Sisodia, R., Wolfe, D., & Sheth, J. (2007). *Firms of endearment.* Upper Saddle River, NJ: Wharton Wharton School Publishing.

Sober, E., & Wilson, D. (1998). *Unto others: The evolution and psychology of unselfish behavior*. Cambridge, MA: Harvard University Press.

Stecher, B. M., Holtzman, D. J., Garet, M. S., Hamilton, L. S., Engberg, J., Steiner, E. D., … Brodziak de los Reyes, I. (2018). *Improving teacher effectiveness: Final report*. Santa Monica, CA: RAND Corporation.

Taylor, F. (2007). *The principles of scientific management.* Charleston, SC: Biblio Bazaar. (Original work published 1911)

von Krogh, G., Ichijo, K., & Nonaka, I. (2000). *Enabling knowledge creation: How to unlock the mystery of tacit knowledge and release the power of innovation.* Oxford, United Kingdom: Oxford University Press.

Williams, J. (2018). *Stand out of our Light: Freedom and Resistance in the Attention Economy.* Cambridge: Cambridge University Press.

Wilson, D. S. (2019). *This view of life.* New York, NY: Pantheon Books.

Wilson, E. O. (2014). *The meaning of human existence.* New York, NY: W.W. Norton.

About the Author

Michael Fullan, OC, is the former Dean of the Ontario Institute for Studies in Education and Professor Emeritus of the University of Toronto. He is co-leader of the New Pedagogies for Deep Learning global initiative (npdl.global). He served as Special Adviser to Ontario Premier Dalton McGuinty from 2003–2013. Recognized as a worldwide authority on educational reform, he advises policy makers and local leaders in helping to achieve the moral purpose of all children learning. Michael Fullan received the Order of Canada in December 2012. He holds honorary doctorates from several universities around the world.

Fullan is a prolific, award-winning author whose books have been published in many languages. The first edition of *Leading in a Culture of Change* was published in 2001 and won the "Book of the Year Award" from Learning Forward. His latest books are *Nuance: Why Some Leaders Succeed and Others Fail*, and *Core Governance* (with Davis Campbell).

For more information on books, articles, videos, and change initiatives around the world, please visit www.michaelfullan.ca.

Acknowledgments

MY THANKS TO JOSSEY-BASS AND ITS EDITORIAL staff for their continued interest and expert support in publishing *Leading in a Culture of Change*. I thank Claudia Cuttress for all her great work in helping to produce everything we do: books, videos, website, workshops, marketing, and more. There is a lot going on and Claudia is a master of orchestrating and producing high quality work on a continuous basis. Underpinning our work is a large, hugely talented, and diverse team that I am blessed to work with—thank you all!

A big thanks to the countless practitioners and policy makers with whom we work. I get my best ideas by being immersed in the daily work of leading practitioners.

I dedicated this book to "wildness lying in wait." Well, the world of leading practitioners is "theory lying in wait." I thank you all for the opportunity to learn. Leading in a culture of change means living in a culture of change—a very rich life, if you are an author.

Index